Mentoring and Professional Review in Waldorf Early Childhood Education

Edited by Diane David

WECAN

WALDORF EARLY CHILDHOOD
ASSOCIATION OF NORTH AMERICA

Spring Valley, New York

Mentoring and Professional Review in Waldorf Early Childhood Education

ISBN 978-1-936849-65-9

This edition comprises two formerly separate works: *Mentoring in Waldorf Early Childhood Education*, edited by Nancy Foster; and *Professional Review in Waldorf Early Childhood Education*, edited by Holly Koteen-Soulé. In publishing this updated omnibus edition, we gratefully acknowledge the work of the WECAN Mentoring Task Force and all the authors and editors.

This publication is made possible by a grant from the Waldorf Curriculum Fund.

Cover art: Richard Neal
Layout and design: Amy Thesing, amythesing.net
The image on page 51 is by Susan Silverio and is used with permission.

Published in the United States by

WECAN
WALDORF EARLY CHILDHOOD
ASSOCIATION OF NORTH AMERICA

The Waldorf Early Childhood Association of North America
285 Hungry Hollow Road
Spring Valley, New York 10977

info@waldorfearlychildhood.org
www.waldorfearlychildhood.org
store.waldorfearlychildhood.org

Contents

Foreword

This updated, expanded volume comprises two books previously published by the Waldorf Early Childhood Association of North America (WECAN): *Mentoring in Waldorf Early Childhood Education* and *Professional Review and Evaluation in Waldorf Early Childhood*. The articles remain a substantial reflection of the original work by the WECAN Mentoring Task Force, named below in Nancy Foster's "Introduction to the First Edition" in 2007. Thank you to Allison Carroll, Louise deForest, and Anna Rainville for their new contributions to this edition.

One of the great gifts of the Waldorf educator is to stimulate the human capacity for lifelong learning. This capacity is nurtured in both the students and their teachers. Rudolf Steiner admonishes us never to be stale, and certainly the children who come to us are asking—indeed, demanding—that we continue to grow and learn. We are grateful to Steiner's insights, which provide the substance for our work and enkindle our enthusiasm.

Much gratitude should be showered on the work of the Mentoring Task Force. Through the mentoring partnership and the evaluation experience, we encourage and support professional growth. Early childhood teaching is a challenging profession, and having a supportive colleague can be a crucial factor in a teacher's developing competency, pedagogical artistry, and self-confidence.

A special thank you to Susan Howard, who spearheaded this project and is always an inspiration to those who work with young children.

These books have been used extensively by many in our Waldorf early childhood movement. I hope that this new edition will support many more fruitful evaluations and mentoring relationships to come.

—Diane David

Introduction to the Omnibus Edition

Diane David

The essence of our human experience is one's relationship with another human being.

When a space can be created between two human beings—a point of stillness, where we listen, speak truth, share, and then come to a new or transformed idea—an enlightening and soul-filled experience takes place.

And this takes some work.

While there may be checklists at the end of this book, there is nothing systematic about this process. To be a Waldorf early childhood teacher, whether experienced or fresh out of a teacher education institute, we know we must always put the child at the center of our work. Around this child we create an ethic of care, open ourselves to create resonance with another, and act out of responsibility.

All of the above must be considered in the mentor and mentee experience or in the encounter of being professionally reviewed. To be in these relationships is to be at once practical and also to reach beyond one's place of comfort. Can we observe and listen with an open heart? Can we accept each other's biographies; can we speak each other's "language"?

Mentorship and professional review are essential for building strong early childhood programs, which are foundational for schools to thrive. Schools must devote time and provide financial resources for the professional development of their teachers.

If there are not enough experienced teachers in a school to provide these services, we can cultivate mentors and evaluators from the wider Waldorf community.

This is investment in the future.

It is my hope that this book provides inspiration and practical ideas for this work together, in sacred relationship with each other and in service of the child.

Blessings on the work ahead.

Part I.
Mentoring in Waldorf Early Childhood Education

Introduction to the First Edition

Along with a growing interest in Waldorf education and the proliferation of new initiatives comes the need for more early childhood teachers and caregivers. And along with the preparation of these professionals—through early childhood education programs and individual inner work—comes the need for collegial support. Such support is of value not only to new teachers and caregivers as they launch into this vital work, but also to those with experience who are seeking further professional development.

Through the mentoring partnership, professional growth of both mentor and mentee are encouraged and supported. Ecclesiastes 4: 9–10 wonderfully expresses the essence of mentoring:

> Two are better than one because they have a good reward for their toil. For if they fall, one will lift up the other, but woe to one who is alone and falls and does not have another to help.

The Mentoring Task Force of WECAN was formed in 2004 in recognition of the essential role of mentoring in the healthy development of Waldorf early childhood education and Waldorf early childhood teachers and caregivers. Our mandate was to find ways to offer support and guidance to those who are mentoring others. In consultation with other experienced Waldorf early childhood mentors from all over North America, we have created a document that we hope will be informative and helpful to mentors, to those who are being mentored, and to schools and other settings that may be establishing in-house mentoring practices.

We offer practical guidelines for clarity in the mentoring process, thoughts on the role of self-education, and a look at the underlying essentials of Waldorf early childhood education. We also include chapters on the nature of advice and on the art of fruitful conversation, which is the heart of the mentoring relationship. The final chapter, an examination of the path of adult learning and self-development, could be a valuable resource for faculty study. A list of references follows the appendix to Part II.

Our intention is to provide a working handbook for the mentoring partnership. Such a handbook is necessarily incomplete, a work in progress. Mentoring, like teaching, involves continual growth, questioning, and learning. We hope this book may play a part in that process.

—Nancy Foster, for the 2007 WECAN Mentoring Task Force:
Nancy Foster, Andrea Gambardella, Susan Howard, Carol Nasr Griset,
Kim Raymond, Celia Riahi, Susan Silverio, and Connie White

Ecclesiastes 4:9 is quoted from the New Revised Standard Version Updated.

1. Self-Education as the Basis for the Art of Mentoring

Andrea Gambardella

Children are coming, and are here! Climate change issues, social and political unrest, and social structures are rapidly changing; everyone is being affected deeply by the benefits and influence of technology. Parents, teachers, and others want a loving world, so they are inspired to open Waldorf playgroups, schools, and care programs to meet these children who want to live into these times. There is a burgeoning need for new Waldorf teachers and care providers. This, in turn, engenders a need for experienced teachers and care providers to support and accompany them on their journey of professional and personal development, while at the same time deepening their own capacities to provide such support.

One tool for meeting the self-development needs of both new and experienced teachers and care providers is the collegial partnership of mentoring. Engaging in a mentoring relationship can provide significant opportunity for mutual growth in terms of both inner reflection and development of practical skills.

The mentor brings to the relationship years of service to children; through experience, they have developed a refined approach to working with young children. How does an experienced teacher offer help and support, while meeting a newer teacher with respect and refraining from a prescriptive approach? How can the experienced teacher enter the mentoring relationship with a prepared inner space to share and work with the other's experiences and inquiry? How can one be an active ingredient in the other's self-education? In short—how does an experienced teacher become an effective mentor?

Those who take up the work of mentoring embrace self-development as an essential part of their professional and personal life. In Waldorf education, such work arises from the wellspring of anthroposophy and the possibilities of inner life practices offered by Rudolf Steiner. A powerful expression of this process of self-development is offered in a verse by Steiner, found in *Verses and Meditations*:

The wishes of the soul are springing,
The deeds of the will are thriving,
The fruits of life are maturing.
I feel my fate,

My fate finds me.
I feel my star,
My star finds me.
I feel my goals in life,
My goals in life are finding me.
My soul and the great World are one.
Life grows more radiant about me,
Life grows more arduous for me,
Grows more abundant within me (Steiner 2005).

The activity of self-development requires strong intention and concerted effort, regardless of what specific inner practices are chosen for daily work. In a lecture of 1912, *Self-Education in the Light of Spiritual Science*, Rudolf Steiner offers us helpful suggestions for cultivating the soul capacities of thinking, feeling, and willing in a way that will support our efforts as mentors toward unprejudiced judgment; toward rising above our sympathies and antipathies; and toward entering the human encounter of the mentoring relationship in a direct and honest way. In this sense of inner work and striving, Rudolf Steiner uses the term "self-education" to indicate that the adult is at the same time both teacher and student (Steiner 1995b).

Cultivating Dynamic Balance

In his lecture on self-education, Steiner describes the self-education of the will through interaction with the outer world. He encourages us to confront people and life situations directly, tempering the brooding tendency of our thoughts and feelings. For the early childhood educator, the activity of the children offers a clue for our own work in the realm of the will:

> In a certain sense, play remains an important educational factor throughout life . . . where we set our muscles in motion, without any deduction . . . then we have a self-educational form of play . . . If we are able through spiritual science to rise up to where the human being can leave his personality without losing himself, then we are educating ourselves by taking hold of life directly. If we let life work on us just as play works on the child (and the comparison should not be misunderstood) then we are educating our will . . . How can we understand this? . . . [T]he human being educates himself best through life experiences which he doesn't understand with his intellect but to which he feels connected in sympathy or love, or a feeling that the things are sublime or touch his sense of humor (Steiner 1995b).

Of course, thinking and feeling are always intertwined with willing, and so we must attend to their education as well, especially regarding their interaction with our deeds and actions. In this lecture, Steiner indicates that we may work with our sympathies and antipathies through reflecting on our emotions and character "with wise self-knowledge." This reflection is not to be attempted while we are under the sway of our emotions, but at a time when we are least influenced by them. Therefore, Steiner says, in addition to meeting the outer world directly, "the will must be educated in life by taking the course of our moods and emotions wisely in hand" (Steiner 1995b). In *How to Know Higher*

Worlds, Rudolf Steiner describes the eightfold path as a practical way to work with meeting the outer world (Steiner 1994). These exercises, also appearing in *Guidance in Esoteric Training* (Steiner 2001) as the exercises for the days of the week, include "right contemplation," giving consideration to the interconnected relationships of thinking, feeling, and action.

What does this mean for the mentor? Considering sympathy and antipathy as two poles, we seek for what lives in the balance. This place of balance may serve as a vessel for a mentor's observations. In Rudolf Steiner's statue of the *Representative of Humanity*,[1] we can see the dynamic gesture through which the two poles are rightfully held in balance so that our highest self can look out into the world as a true human being. This dynamic balance might be schooled by engaging in artistic activity where one can meet and work with inner mobility.

While a variety of experience and interaction educates our will, quiet moments of review help us to school our feeling life. Taking a walk, journaling, or carving out time to sit quietly are some pathways for such reflection. Developing our cognitive faculties requires the active focus of concentration. As Rudolf Steiner states in the 1912 lecture, "Whoever has managed to reduce things (thoughts, impressions, perceptions) to certain main ideas will find that he can confront life with great serenity when it demands active deeds from him" (Steiner 1995b). As an experienced early childhood teacher, the mentor practices this principle of concentration and focus in creating the classroom environment and the rhythms of activity and rest. Simplicity, expressed by the wise saying, "Less is more," reigns as a cornerstone of caring for young children, and so, the mentor may bring this same practice into the mentoring relationship. This practice of concentration provides the mentor with a lens for observations and for creating a sense of direction for the encounter with the mentee. This concentration on essentials arises out of attentiveness: directing and acknowledging the focus of our attention; being fully present.

Making Way for Something New

In addition to developing and strengthening our cognitive capacities, honing our ability to focus our attention bears other fruit for the mentor. In his lecture on self-education, Steiner describes the aspects of our thinking capacity: to remember, picture, and "forget in the right way."

In this context, "forgetting" indicates a release or letting go of an image or thought content, thus creating a space into which something new can enter. Rudolf Steiner describes such a process in some detail as a part of the Rose Cross meditation, found in chapter 5 of *An Outline of Esoteric Science* (Steiner 1997).

In this exercise, an image is carefully built up in thought, imbued with feeling, and then extinguished. This is the point at which the true meditation begins, and the possibility for communion with a higher world begins to exist. Another process of release is offered in the "Review of the Day" or *Rückshau*, in which details are remembered, visualized, and then allowed to dissolve (Steiner 2001).

---

1   In this statue, Rudolf Steiner shows the universal human being standing between the opposing forces of Lucifer and Ahriman, holding them in dynamic balance. Originally intended for the first Goetheanum, the *Representative of Humanity* now stands in the second Goetheanum in Dornach, Switzerland. Images are available online.

As mentors we carry our extensive professional experiences with us. In this process of "forgetting," we may find clues for extinguishing what we have built up with effort, love, and care, so that we may allow what is new—and truly needed—to arise in the mentoring encounter.

In our teaching, we know how to order the children's environment and rhythms of activity; these are transparent for the child's imitation, meaningful gestures that require no accompanying words. In mentoring, however, there is no prescription for the mentee to simply imitate us like a child, nor, as an adult, to understand us simply by listening to our reports of our own practices. Therefore, before entering the classroom of our mentee, we allow our carefully built-up concepts of "how things are done" to dissolve, so that the possibility is created for something altogether new to appear.

In his guidance on self-education, Steiner tells us that out of what we have forgotten, there often arises something imagined, a fantasy, that fuels our creativity. Whatever we do to move our soul forces to creativity brings fruit to our work and promotes life (Steiner 2001).

Mentoring and Destiny

Finally, Rudolf Steiner brings to our attention the essential acknowledgment of our destiny as an ingredient in self-education. We learn the right way to move between passive surrender and active engagement in life as key elements of this acknowledgment. The effort required for the practice of acknowledging our destiny and being awake in our life-encounters allows us to reach beyond the boundaries of our own personality. Steiner points to the capacity for compassion—the experience of another's pain or joy—as one result of such efforts to transcend our boundaries. In compassion, the mentor acknowledges moments of struggle and of success, recognizing that such moments belong to the path of personal and professional development for all teachers and care providers. The mentor is enabled to hold with respect the destiny questions carried by the mentee.

One who lives in acknowledgement of destiny can be assured that the Self, which transcends the ordinary self and guides us in our life's purpose, has brought about the mentoring relationship. Acknowledgement of destiny allows the mentor to approach their relationship to mentee with calm composure and a sense of devotion (Steiner 1995b).

Looking far back in history, we can be reminded of the roots of our work as mentors. In the story of the Odyssey, we are told that Odysseus, in setting out for Troy, entrusted his house and the education of his son Telemachus to his friend Mentor. Thus, the mentor is not merely someone who offers experience and skill, but is also a trusted confidant. The elements of love, dedication, and trustworthiness are inherent in the essence of mentoring.

2. *Laying the Basis for the Mentoring Visit*

Nancy Foster

This chapter offers a look at the practical aspects of preparing for the mentoring visit. Establishing an open, trusting mentoring relationship is essential to a fruitful experience for both mentor and mentee, and getting off on the right foot can do much toward establishing such trust. Clarity of purpose, transparency of process, and mutual understanding of the approach to observation and follow-up will all contribute to a healthy working relationship. What follows, therefore, is a nuts-and-bolts approach to the mentoring visit.

CLARITY OF EXPECTATIONS

Mentoring for an Early Childhood Education Program

In mentoring for an educational program, it is helpful if the program director gives a written statement to both the mentor and mentee outlining expectations for the mentoring visits, including the following.

- purpose of the visit (aspects to be observed; an observation form may be provided)
- length of meeting/conversation time to follow the observation
- format of the observation record and how/with whom it is to be shared
- responsibilities of the mentee in terms of housing, parking, meals, time and space for conversation

A mentor for a training program does not provide a record for, or meet with, any committee or other representative of the mentee's school or center. Their responsibility is solely to the mentee and the training program. If the mentee wishes to share the record with their school or center, they may do so.

15

Independently Requested Mentoring

In mentoring requested by a teacher or caregiver or their school or center, the above factors also need to be clearly agreed upon before the mentor's visit. If a written statement of expectations for the mentor is not provided, they should request such a statement or possibly draft one and offer it as the basis for an agreement.

A statement of agreement should include whether someone in addition to the teacher or caregiver, such as an in-school mentor or pedagogical director, is to receive a record of the visit, and in what form it will be presented (written? a meeting with a committee or individual?). The purpose of the mentoring visit, as well as whether an element of evaluation is to be included, should be clear both to the mentor and the mentee.

Compensation for the Mentor

Mentoring is carried out for the deepening and health of the Waldorf movement, and care must be taken to find the appropriate level of compensation depending on circumstances. Some mentors may have to take time off from their program; others may be retired or on sabbatical. Travel expenses may be a factor. Early childhood teacher education programs generally have an established daily honorarium for mentoring, plus a provision for reimbursing travel expenses. If a mentor is engaged by a school or center, the daily rate established by AWSNA and WECAN may serve as a guide. In any case, extra obligations taken on by the mentor (such as an evening talk for parents) should be arranged separately with the school or center at an additional fee.

PRACTICAL PREPARATIONS FOR THE VISIT

The mentor should contact the mentee before the visit to arrange or confirm the date and time of the visit and other details of the arrangements. It is worthwhile for the mentor to request the following information in writing before the visit.

- class demographics (size and age range of group)
- daily and weekly rhythm of the class

The mentor may request additional information from the mentee, which might take the form of a self-evaluation.

- aspects of the work that the mentee feels are their strengths
- any particular areas of concern to the mentee; this could include pedagogical questions, particular children, collegial relationships, or other aspects of challenge

Both kinds of information will prepare the mentor to be attuned to the content and context of the observation.

The mentee should make arrangements in advance to ensure that there is a protected time and space conducive to a fruitful conversation after the observation. Whether to include the classroom colleague in the conversation should also be considered. In some situations, it may be helpful to include the colleague for part of the time but it is also essential that the mentor and mentee have adequate time for private conversation.

Mutually agreeable arrangements will need to be made for travel, meals, and housing. Possibilities for housing might include staying with the mentee, with another faculty member, or with a parent, taking into account any allergies or other considerations.

It is helpful for the mentor and mentee to discuss by phone or email before the visit what the mentor's role in the classroom will be during the visit. Is there work the mentee would like the mentor to help with, or should they bring their own handwork? Should the mentor participate in any of the morning activities or simply sit and observe? The two should agree on what will be most helpful and comfortable for both parties. (See additional details in chapter 4.)

ESTABLISHING TRUST AND RAPPORT

It is helpful for the mentor to remind the mentee that they are coming to offer support for the mentee's striving as a professional, not to judge their work. The mentor is visiting in the spirit of "How can we work together to support your growth as a teacher or caregiver?" They may ask, "Is there anything I can help you with?"

If time allows, a face-to-face conversation before the actual observation can be helpful, to give the mentor and mentee time to get acquainted if they have not met before, and permit the mentor to gain a sense of the mentee's circumstances and state of being. Learning something of the mentee's interests and joys beyond the world of work can help to create a personal connection. This connection can be deepened if the mentor shares their own biography. If such a conversation is not possible, the preparatory phone conversation described above can help to meet this need. Other possibilities for forming a social relationship between mentor and mentee include a home visit, going for a walk, or having dinner together, depending on circumstances.

During the conversation following the observation, the mentee usually feels more comfortable if the mentor does not give the sense that there is "one right way" and that the mentee will be judged by that standard. Rather, it will help build the mentee's confidence if the mentor clearly makes an effort to understand what they are trying to do and works with them on that basis. The mentor's openness to a particular situation (for example, if the mentee is working in a public school or other non-Waldorf setting) will be a positive contribution. Additionally, the mentor will want to be sensitive to how the mentee was trained and the philosophy and policies of the educational institution.

A sense of trust and rapport are created when the mentor is a good listener and responds thoughtfully to what they hear, rather than lecturing the mentee, and when positive comments are freely offered.

Mutually supportive colleagueship can be built if the mentor shares their own questions and struggles with the mentee, rather than delivering a series of "shoulds" and "should nots." The mentor will need to use restraint and discretion in sharing experiences, choosing only relevant events that will really help the mentee.

It can also be helpful if the mentor asks questions, such as, "What was your intention when you [removed Billy from the painting table]?" or "Was the transition from circle time to snack typical today?" or "How do you feel the children are affected when you arrive at the same time as they do in the morning?" It is sometimes useful for the mentor to restate what the mentee has said, to help the mentee perceive whether they have really said what they meant and, if so, whether the mentor has understood. Chapter 5 discusses the mentoring conversation in depth.

THE MENTOR'S PREPARATION FOR THE VISIT

Before the observation, the mentor may review the information the mentee has offered: the composition of the class, the morning rhythm, and the mentee's statement of their perceived strengths and questions or concerns. If the mentor has previously observed this mentee, they may wish to reread their observations of that visit; or they may prefer to do this after the observation so as to begin with a "clean slate," while afterwards bringing to consciousness those areas where change has occurred. The mentor may also wish to reacquaint themself with any observation criteria established by the mentee's training program.

Meditative preparation by the mentor on the evening and/or morning preceding the observation helps to lay the basis for a perceptive eye, an understanding heart, and a tactful yet honest approach to the conversation that follows the observation. There are, of course, many possibilities for such preparation, and this must be left to the freedom of the mentor. A valuable collection of meditative material is found in *Spiritual Insights*, compiled from Rudolf Steiner's work by Helmut von Kügelgen and published by WECAN (Steiner 2013a). This and other sources are listed in the references.

In summary, a successful mentoring visit—one that helps and supports the mentee in their development—begins with clear mutual expectations, a sharing of preliminary information, the establishment of a trusting relationship, and inner preparation on the part of the mentor.

3. *The Essentials of Waldorf Early Childhood Education*

Susan Howard

Is there a Waldorf early childhood "curriculum?" Are there specific activities—perhaps puppet plays or watercolor painting, for example—that are required in a Waldorf program? Are there certain materials and furnishings—lazured, soft-colored walls, handmade playthings, natural materials, beeswax crayons—that are essential ingredients of a Waldorf setting? What is it that makes Waldorf early childhood education "Waldorf?" Rudolf Steiner spoke on a number of occasions about the essentials of education and of early childhood education. His words shed light on what he considered fundamental:

> Essentially, there is no education other than self-education, whatever the level may be. This is recognized in its full depth within Anthroposophy, which has conscious knowledge through spiritual investigation of repeated Earth lives. Every education is self-education, and as teachers we can only provide the environment for children's self-education. We have to provide the most favorable conditions where, through our agency, children can educate themselves according to their own destinies. This is the attitude that teachers should have toward children, and such an attitude can be developed only through an ever-growing awareness of this fact (Steiner 1996b, 141).

Thus the essential element in early childhood education is actually the educator, who shapes and influences the children's environment, not only through the furnishings, activities, and rhythms of the day, but most important, through the qualities of their own being and relationships: with the children and other adults in the kindergarten or early childhood setting, with the parents, to daily life in the kindergarten, and to living on earth.

These qualities, which include attitudes and gestures both outer and inner, permeate the early childhood setting and deeply influence the children, who take them up through a process of imitation. The results of such experiences appear much later in the child's life through predispositions, tendencies, and attitudes toward life's opportunities and challenges.

Viewed in this way, early childhood education demands an ongoing process of self-education by the adult. If we again ask, what makes a Waldorf program "Waldorf," the answers might be sought less in the particular activities or rhythms or materials and furnishings, and more in the extent to which these outer aspects are harmonious expressions of inner qualities, attitudes, capacities, and intentions of the teacher—all of which can have a health-giving effect on the children, both in the moment and for the rest of their lives.

Those of us who are committed to this path of Waldorf early childhood education, whether as early childhood teachers or mentors, may actively ask ourselves how qualities essential to the healthy development of young children are living in our own early childhood groups, in our own daily lives, and in our own inner practice.

Rudolf Steiner spoke on a number of occasions about experiences essential for healthy early childhood education, including the following:

- Love and warmth
- Care for the environment and nourishment for the senses
- Creative, artistic experience
- Meaningful adult activity as an example for the child's imitation
- Free, imaginative play
- Protection for the forces of childhood
- Gratitude, reverence, and wonder
- Joy, humor, and happiness
- Adult caregivers on a path of inner development

The following brief descriptions of these qualities and related questions are intended to serve the self-reflection of the individual teacher, the observations of the mentor, and the process of helpful, open dialogue between mentor and mentee.

Love and Warmth

> Children who live in . . . an atmosphere of love and warmth, and who have around them truly good examples to imitate, are living in their proper element (Steiner 1996b, 22).

Love and warmth, more than any programmatic approach to early education, create the basis for development. These qualities are expressed in the gestures that live between adult and child, in the children's behavior toward one another, and also in the social relations among the adults in the early childhood center. In other words, they form the social community of early childhood education and can foster a sense of belonging. When Rudolf Steiner visited the classes of the first Waldorf school, he was known to ask the school children, "Do you love your teacher?"

Questions we can ask ourselves and discuss in mentoring conversations include the following:

- Are love and warmth living in the atmosphere?
- How are they expressed in the gestures that live between adult and child?
- How are they expressed in the children's behavior toward one another?
- How are the social relations among the adults caring for the children?
- What hindrances exist to creating a loving atmosphere?
- How is love expressed in the teacher's response to "inappropriate" behavior (excessive noise, aggression, disruptions, conflict)?

Less apparent within the day, but also of great significance, are these same qualities of love and warmth in relations with colleagues outside the classroom, with the parents, and with the wider community:

- How are the relations between the early childhood educators and the parents?
- How are the relations with the other colleagues in the early childhood groups and in the rest of the school?
- How does the teacher work with conflict and difficulties with adults?
- Are the children surrounded by a community that offers love and warmth and support?

Care for the Environment and Nourishment for the Senses

> The essential task of the kindergarten teacher is to create the proper physical environment around the children . . . "Physical environment" must be understood in the widest sense imaginable. It includes not just what happens around children in the material sense, but everything that occurs in their environment—everything that can be perceived by their senses, that can work on the inner powers of children from the surrounding physical space. This includes all moral or immoral actions, all the meaningful and meaningless behaviors that children witness (Steiner 1996b, 18).

Early learning is profoundly connected to the child's own physical body and sensory experience. Thus the physical surroundings, indoors and outdoors, should provide nourishing, diverse opportunities for the child's active self-education. By integrating diverse elements and bringing them into a meaningful, understandable and harmonious order, the adult provides surroundings that are accessible to the young child's understanding, feeling, and active will. Such surroundings provide the basis for the development of a sense of coherence. The child unconsciously experiences the love, care, intentions, and consciousness expressed through the *outer* furnishings and materials of the classroom. The *inner* qualities offer a moral grounding for the child's development; the environment is "ensouled" and nurturing.

The adult shapes not only the spatial environment, but also the temporal environment, creating a loving, lively yet orderly "breathing" through rhythm and repetition. Through this healthy breathing process, the child gains a sense of security and confidence in their relationship with the world.

Here we can ask:

- Does the environment of the early childhood program offer these qualities of order, care, transparency, and meaning? What is expressed through the outer furnishings and materials?

- Does the space offer diverse opportunities for nourishing experiences in the realm of touch, self-movement, balance, and well-being?

- Are the activities of the day integrated in time into a healthy flow, in which transitions are as smooth and seamless as possible?

- Are there opportunities for lively, joyful physical movement as well as for more inward, listening experience? for large-group, small-group, and solitary experiences?

Creative, Artistic Experience

[I]n order to become true educators, the essential thing is to be able to see the truly aesthetic element in the work, to bring an artistic quality into our tasks. . . . If we bring this aesthetic element, we then begin to come closer to what the child wills out of its own nature (Steiner 2012, 30).

In the early childhood class, the art of education is the art of living. Teachers are artists in how they perceive and relate to the children and the activities of daily life. The educator "orchestrates" and "choreographs" the rhythms of each day, the week, and the seasons in such a way that the children can breathe freely within a living structure. In addition, the educator offers the children opportunities for artistic experiences through song and instrumental music, movement and gesture (including rhythmic games and eurythmy), speech and language (including verses, poetry, and stories), modeling, watercolor painting and drawing, puppetry and marionettes.

Here we may ask:

- How do the arts live in the kindergarten, in the teacher, and in the children?

- How is the rhythmic flow of time formed?

- Is the teacher engaged artistically in the domestic arts and work processes?

- How is creative, artistic experience of the child fostered through the furnishings and play materials of the kindergarten?

- Is the play of the children creative and artistic in its imagery, its social interactions, its processes?

- Is the teacher's work with individual children both practical and imaginative? What kinds of imaginations inform their work?

- Is the teacher engaged in creative artistic endeavors? Are they striving to deepen their own understanding and experience of what it means to be artistic?

Meaningful Adult Activity as an Example for the Child's Imitation

The task of the kindergarten teacher is to adapt the practical activities of daily life so that they are suitable for the child's imitation through play. . . . The activities of children in kindergarten must be derived directly from life itself rather than being "thought out" by the intellectualized culture of adults. In the kindergarten, the most important thing is to give children the opportunity to directly imitate life itself (Steiner 1996a, 72).

Children do not learn through instruction or admonition, but through imitation. . . . Good sight will develop if the environment has the proper conditions of light and color, while in the brain and blood circulation, the physical foundations will be laid for a healthy sense of morality if children witness moral actions in their surroundings (Steiner 1996b, 19).

Real, meaningful, purposeful work, adjusted to the needs of the child, is in accordance with the child's natural and inborn need for activity and is an enormously significant educational activity. Thus, rather than offering contrived projects and activities for the children, educators focus on their own meaningful work through activities that nurture daily and seasonal life in the classroom "home": cooking and baking, gardening, laundry and cleaning, creating and caring for the materials in the surroundings, and the bodily care of the children.

This creates a realm, an atmosphere, of freedom in which the individuality of each child can be active. It is not intended that the children copy the outer movements and actions of the adult, but rather that they experience the inner work attitude: the devotion, care, sense of purpose, intensity of focus, and creative spirit of the adult. And then, in turn, each child is free to act as an artist-doer in their own right, through creative free play and active movement, according to their own inner needs and possibilities.

As we observe an early childhood class, we may ask ourselves:

- How does meaningful adult activity live in the group, both indoors and out?

- Do the educators seem able to devote themselves inwardly and outwardly with enthusiasm, in an artistic way, to real life activities and adult work?

- Does the educator appear engaged artistically in a creative process?

- Are the educators' activities truly meaningful and purposeful, in a logical sequence that the child can grasp?

- Do the children imitate the adult's work through their play (not necessarily the outer actions, but perhaps more importantly through the inner gesture of the adult's work)?

- What qualities are expressed in the children's play?

Free, Imaginative Play

In the child's play activity, we can only provide the conditions for education. What is gained through play stems fundamentally from the self-activity of the child, through everything that cannot be determined by fixed rules. The real educational value of play lies in the fact that we ignore our rules and regulations, our educational theories, and allow the child free rein (Steiner 1995b).

And then, a seemingly contradictory indication:

Giving direction and guidance to play is one of the essential tasks of sensible education, which is to say of an art of education that is right for humanity. . . . Early childhood educators must school their own observation in order to develop an artistic eye, to detect the individual quality of each child's play (Steiner 2012, 32).

Little children learn through play. They approach play in an entirely individual way, out of their own unique configuration of soul and spirit, and out of their own unique experiences in the world they live in. In addition, the manner in which each child plays may offer a picture of how they will take up their destiny as an adult.

The task of the early childhood educator is to create an environment that supports the possibility for healthy play. This environment includes the physical surroundings, furnishings, and play materials; the social environment of activities and social interactions; and the inner/spiritual environment of thoughts, intentions, and imaginations held by the adults.

We may ask the following questions relating to the children's play in the kindergarten or early childhood setting:

- What is the quality and duration of the children's play? Is it active, dynamic, healthy, creative? Are the children self-directed and deeply engaged, socially and individually?

- How does the early childhood educator reconcile these two seemingly contradictory challenges: to give free rein to the child at play, and to guide and direct and provide the conditions for healthy play to develop?

- What are the themes and images of free play?

- Do the play materials offer diverse and open-ended possibilities for creativity, social interaction, and bodily movement?

- Are there opportunities for a wide range of play activities outdoors? How are the children active outdoors, compared with indoors? How much time is there for indoor vs. outdoor play?

Protection for the Forces of Childhood

Although it is highly necessary that each person should be fully awake in later life, the child must be allowed to remain as long as possible in the peaceful, dreamlike condition of pictorial imagination in which his early years of life are passed. For if we allow the child's organism to grow strong in this non-intellectual way, they will rightly develop in later life the intellectuality needed in the world today (Steiner 2012, 31).

The lively, waking dream of the little child's consciousness must be allowed to thrive in the early childhood group. This means that the educator refrains as much as possible from verbal instruction; instead, their gestures and actions provide a model for the child's imitation, and familiar rhythms and activities provide a context where the need for verbal instruction is reduced. Simple, archetypal imagery in stories, songs, and games provides "digestible" experiences that do not require intellectual or critical reflection or explanation.

Here we may ask ourselves as educators:

- Does the atmosphere in the room foster an imaginative, not-yet intellectually awakened consciousness in the children?

- Are the children allowed to immerse themselves fully in play without unnecessary instruction and verbal direction from the adults?

- Are play processes allowed to run their course, or are they interrupted?

- Does a "group consciousness" prevail in group activities, or are children singled out for special privileges and "turns" and offered choices?

- Do the sequence and rhythms of the day carry the children along, or do the children ask what is coming next?

- Does the educator invite children to participate in activities such as rhythmic circles or finger games through their own activity, or do they wait to see if children are "ready" or verbally explain what is coming?

An Atmosphere of Gratitude, Reverence, and Wonder

An atmosphere of gratitude should grow naturally in children through merely witnessing the gratitude the adults feel as they receive what is freely given by others, and in how they express this gratitude . . . If a child says "thank you" very naturally—not in response to the urging of others, but simply through imitating—something has been done that will greatly benefit the child's whole life. Out of this an all-embracing gratitude will develop toward the whole world. This cultivation of gratitude is of paramount importance (Steiner 1996a, 125–26).

Out of these early all-pervading experiences of gratitude, the first tender capacity for love, which is deeply embedded in each and every child, begins to sprout in earthly life.

If, during the first period of life, we create an atmosphere of gratitude around the children . . . then out of this gratitude toward the world, toward the entire universe, and also out of thankfulness for being able to be in this world . . . a profound and warm sense of devotion will arise . . . upright, honest and true (ibid.).

This is the basis for what will become a capacity for deep, intimate love and commitment in later life, for dedication and loyalty, for true admiration of others, for fervent spiritual or religious devotion, and for placing oneself wholeheartedly in the service of the world.

And so we may ask:

- How do gratitude, reverence, and wonder live in the kindergarten?
- Do they come to natural expression from adults and children?
- Are they spontaneous and sincere, or sentimentalized?
- Or if these qualities seem to be missing, how does their absence manifest?

Joy, Humor, and Happiness

The joy of children in and with their environment must therefore be counted among the forces that build and shape the physical organs. They need teachers who look and act with happiness and, most of all, with honest, unaffected love. Such a love that streams, as it were, with warmth through the physical environment of the children may be said to literally "hatch out" the forms of the physical organs (Steiner 1996b, 22).

If you make a surly face so that a child gets the impression you are a grumpy person, this harms the child for the rest of its life. What kind of school plan you make is neither here nor there; what matters is what sort of person you are (Steiner 1995a, 19).

Here we may explore the following questions as educators:

- Do happiness and joy live in this group of children and adults?
- What are the most joy-filled aspects of the work?
- Which aspects of the work are least permeated with joy?
- How is the educator's earnestness and serious striving held in a dynamic balance with humor, happiness, and "honest, unaffected love?"
- Are there moments of laughter and delight in the room? How does humor live in the community of children and adults?

Adult Caregivers on a Path of Inner Development

For the small child before the change of teeth, the most important thing in education is the teacher's own being (Steiner 2019, 14).

Just think what feelings arise in the soul of the early childhood educator who realizes: what I accomplish with this child, I accomplish for the grown-up person in his twenties. What matters is not so much a knowledge of abstract educational principles or pedagogical rules . . . . What does matter is that a deep sense of responsibility develops in our hearts and minds and affects our world view and the way we stand in life (Steiner 2012, 33).

Here we come to the spiritual environment of the early childhood setting: the thoughts, attitudes, and imaginations living in the adult who cares for the children. This invisible realm that lies behind the outer actions of the educator has a profound influence on the child's development.

The spiritual environment includes recognition of the child as a threefold being—of body, soul and spirit—on a path of evolutionary development through repeated earth lives. This recognition provides a foundation for the daily activities in the kindergarten and for the relationship between adult and child.

In addition to the questions we have already pondered above, we may ask:

- How is the adult actively engaged in inner development, as an early childhood educator and as a human being?

- How is the educator cultivating a relationship to the children on a spiritual basis?

- How is the educator working with colleagues to foster an environment of spiritual striving and a deepened study of child and human development?

- Does the educator strive to approach their work in such a way that the children in their care are not burdened by unresolved issues in the educator's personal life?

- Do goodness and moral uprightness stream from the being of the teacher? Is their inner and outer activity in coherence with healthy social and ethical values? Is the educator striving to be an example worthy of the children's imitation?

- Does the educator love the children? Do they work to create healthy, caring relationships with the parents, with colleagues, and with the community? Do they love the earth, and the world into which the children are incarnating?

- How does the educator see their own relationship to the past, the present, and the future of our human journey?

This is the very challenging realm of self-knowledge and the activity of the individual ego of the adult—a realm where it is difficult to be objective in our observations. Yet ultimately it is this realm that may affect the development of the children most profoundly. It is not merely our outer activity that affects the developing child; it is what lies behind and is expressed through this outer activity. Ultimately the most profound influence on the child is who we are as human beings—and who and how we are becoming.

Conclusion

The so-called "essentials" described here are qualitative in nature. For the most part, they do not characterize a body of "best practices"; instead, they describe inner qualities and attributes of the adult that foster healthy development in young children. These qualities can come to expression in a wide variety of ways, according to the age range and particular characteristics of the children in a particular group; the nature of the particular program (a kindergarten or playgroup or extended care program, for example); or the environment and surroundings (urban or rural, home or school or child care center, for example).

Many practices that have come to be associated with Waldorf early childhood education—certain rhythms and rituals, play materials, songs, stories, even the colors of the walls or the dress of the adults or the menu for snack—may be mistakenly taken as essentials. The results of such assumptions can be a "King Winter" nature table appearing in a tropical climate in "wintertime," or having only dolls with pink skin and yellow hair. Such practices may express a tendency toward a doctrinal or dogmatic approach that is out of touch with the realities of the immediate situation and instead imposes something from "outside."

There is a parallel concern at the other end of the spectrum from the doctrinal or dogmatic. The freedom that Waldorf education offers each individual teacher to determine the practices of their early childhood program can be misinterpreted to mean that "anything goes," according to their own personal preferences and style. Here too there is the danger that the developmental realities and needs of the children are not sufficiently taken into consideration.

Each of these one-sided approaches may be injurious to the development of the children. As Waldorf early childhood educators, we are constantly seeking a middle, universally human path between polarities. Rudolf Steiner's advice to the first Waldorf kindergarten teacher, Elizabeth Grunelius, in the early 1920s, could be paraphrased as follows: Observe the children. Actively meditate. Follow your intuitions. Work out of imitation.

Today we are challenged to engage in a constant process of renewal as Waldorf early childhood educators, actively observing today's children in our care, carrying them in our meditations, and seeking to work consciously and artistically to create the experiences that will serve their development. Our devotion to this task awakens us to the importance of self-education and transformation in the context of community. Our ongoing study of child and human development, our own artistic and meditative practices, and our work with anthroposophy, independently and together with others, become essential elements for the practice of Waldorf early childhood education. Here we can come to experience that we are not alone on this journey; we are supported through our encounters with one other and with spiritual beings offering support toward our continued development and toward the renewal of culture Waldorf education seeks to serve.

4. The Mentoring Observation: What Do We Look For?

Nancy Foster

Basic Considerations

In the observation, fundamental questions confront the mentor: What makes a classroom situation "Waldorf?" How do I discern the middle ground in the polarity of relativism (supremacy of individual style or preference) and dogmatism (fundamentalism; the "one right way")? For example, the mentor visits on painting day and notices that the mentee "demonstrates," painting a picture while the children watch. Perhaps the mentor says, "It's inappropriate for the teacher to paint first. This is not the Waldorf way for early childhood." The mentee responds, "But I love to paint, and I've always done it this way. It just feels right to me." In this exchange the mentor is approaching the situation dogmatically, while the mentee is approaching it out of their personal preference. In such a case, a "middle ground" would be based on neither personal preference nor a dogmatic statement, but rather on a mutual exploration of child development and the nature and purpose of the activity of painting. Through such an exploration, an understanding might better be reached. The search for this middle ground can only truly take place in the meeting of the mentor and mentee striving together in a process of becoming. An attitude of warm objectivity during the observation will be helpful to the mentor in resisting the impulse to form quick judgments. Chapter 3, "The Essentials of Waldorf Early Childhood Education," offers both mentors and mentees a valuable basis for considering pedagogical questions.

A mood of honest questioning and seeking on the part of the mentor will contribute to this sense of warm objectivity. The mentor may ask, for example, in response to their own reaction to what is observed, "How do I know whether something is developmentally appropriate?" Such a question may require research. The mentor may suggest that they, along with the mentee, look into the question in preparation for the mentor's next visit, and might suggest sources for this research. The mentor may also strive to see the value in a particular activity, asking, "What was the teacher's intention in this situation?" Such an attitude will add to the value of the conversation to come.

29

The Mentor as Observer: Onlooker or Participant?

An additional question is that of the role of the mentor in the classroom during the observation. Will the mentor learn the most through the "fly on the wall" method, or is participation in the classroom process more conducive to a helpful view of the situation? What role will be most harmonious and least intrusive for the children? There is probably no single answer to this question; rather, it will depend on the particular individuals and situation involved.

While the mentor will not want to sit with notebook and pen in hand, looking on as a clinical observer, they may find it helpful to take unobtrusive notes now and then. The mentor should let the mentee know that this may happen. On the other hand, becoming immersed in the classroom activities might prevent the mentor from taking in a sense of the whole, and direct involvement with the children might be a distraction from observation. In many situations, the middle ground may be that the mentor is busy with simple handwork, playing a part of the "work of the home," while remaining free to attend to what is happening in a given moment. Ironing, for example, is a non-distracting activity that allows the mentor an overview of the classroom.

There may be situations in which the mentee has asked in advance for guidance and the mentor has agreed to take part in an activity as an example. The mentor may, for instance, have brought a rhythmic circle game to lead, or perhaps will take a place at the baking table. In a rare case, a mentor may feel it necessary to intervene in a situation without prior arrangement, but this would occur only in a situation where children are actually at serious risk. Such a case would obviously need to be a topic in the conversation that follows the morning in the classroom.

Observing the Mentor

It can be very helpful for a mentee to visit the mentor's classroom for a morning, if this can be arranged. While conversations offer a wonderful opportunity for mutual learning, and the possibility to address questions together, the value of a deed cannot be overstated. It can happen that a mentee who is teaching while enrolled in a part-time training has never seen a teacher or classroom outside their own school. To observe their mentor or another experienced teacher or caregiver can be most enlightening, stimulating, and inspiring. In some part-time training programs, a mentee's visit to the mentor may be substituted for one of the mentoring visits.

Mentoring an Assistant

If the mentee is an assistant, it is most appropriate for the mentor to focus on the mentee's role rather than the lead teacher's. This will require tact, if the mentee or mentor has questions or concerns about the lead teacher's approach to the work, about decisions they have made concerning the daily rhythm, room arrangement, materials, and so on. The mentor will wish to maintain professionalism and avoid discussing the lead teacher with the assistant.

One approach to this situation is to encourage the assistant to ask questions of the lead teacher in an effort to understand the intention behind the choices the lead teacher has made. Non-critical questions, honestly asked, may help both the assistant and lead teacher to think together and possibly to reach new insights. At the very least, the assistant will come to understand the situation better. It may help the mentee to know that there is much to be learned in any situation, from the children as well as the lead teacher, which will help in the future when the mentee becomes a lead teacher or caregiver.

If the assistant is having serious personal difficulties with the lead teacher, and has been unable to ease the situation through communication with their colleague, the mentor may consider helping to arrange for someone in the school to work with them. This could be the chair of the College of Teachers, or another experienced person on the faculty whom both teachers trust.

THE OBSERVATION: WHAT ARE WE LOOKING FOR?

Possible Criteria for Observation

There are a number of ways to list and organize criteria for observation. Factors to consider might include the following, with the understanding that the mentor may include additional observations and omit any not noted during the visit.

- physical environment: aesthetic quality, arrangement of space, care of the room and storage areas, quality and care of play materials

- role and being of the teacher or caregiver: dress and appearance, physical and moral uprightness, relationship with children and classroom colleague, interaction with parents, mood, presence of a smile, use of voice and speech, quality of selflessness and ego presence, consciousness in relation to time (focused in the moment but aware of the stream of time)

- children: energy level, development of the four lower senses, mood, quality of creative play, participation in the morning rhythm and activities, health, dress, relationship with teacher(s) or caregiver(s), quality of social interactions, care of play materials

- elements of the program's morning or day: daily rhythm, transitions, festival life and relation with nature, mood or atmosphere (gratitude and reverence, joy, humor)

- activities of the day: creative play, clean-up, snack, circle, domestic activities, watercolor painting, story, etc.; developmental appropriateness of activities

- inner work of the adult: extent of self-knowledge and self-evaluation, carrying deep questions; on what resources do they draw?

Intuitive Perception

Alongside a more or less detailed set of criteria that can serve as the basis for observation, there needs to be room for a certain level of intuitive perception on the part of the mentor. The mentor may find it useful, after the observation and before the conversation, to "step back" inwardly and wait to see what impressions may arise. This is a way of finding the middle ground between the "trees" and the "forest"—neither getting caught up in details without a sense of the whole, nor reaching only general impressions that lack specifics.

Discernment of Qualities: A Context of Triads or Polarities

As an aid to discerning and expressing the intangible or inner qualities of the classroom situation and the mentee's work, the mentor may consider triads—two extremes and a middle—and ask where or in what circumstances these qualities have occurred. For example, in considering the mentee's relationship with the children, the mentor might consider the triad of coldness–love out of interest–sentimental warmth. The mentor might observe, for example, that the mentee greets the children upon arrival with a warmth bordering on sentimentality (excessive warmth). In interactions during creative play, the mentee may show warm objectivity or love out of interest, and so on. Another example of a triad, in regard to the care of the environment, might be compulsive orderliness–practical and aesthetic attention to detail–heedlessness or carelessness. By directing the attention to two extremes and a middle way, this approach to observation avoids the good/bad or either/or syndromes, and provides a stimulating basis for collegial discussion and conversation in the meeting following the observation. Not every observation may lend itself to the use of triads, but their consideration may add depth and a seed quality to some aspects of the observation and conversation.

Following are examples of triads that might be considered. These are only examples; an observant mentor will find others.

Physical Environment

CARE OF ROOM

Heedlessness, carelessness	Practical and aesthetic attention to detail	Compulsive orderliness

ARRANGEMENT OF SPACE

Insufficient division of space, inviting aimless or chaotic movement	Functional and welcoming	Room overcrowded, impeding movement

QUALITY OF PLAY MATERIALS

In poor repair, too many, lack of variety	Varied in function, inviting fantasy play and constructive use	"Precious," detailed, highly specific in function

ESTHETIC QUALITY

Unharmonious, lack of care, unfinished appearance	Simple, functional, natural beauty	"Pretty," sentimental, overly decorated

Role and Being of the Adult

QUALITY OF SPEECH

Careless diction, poor grammar, too-soft or too-loud voice	Clear diction, correct grammar, natural tone of voice	Affected, unnatural pronunciation

USE OF LANGUAGE

Frequent talking, asking children questions, offering explanations	Judicious use of speech	Avoidance of speech, failure to respond to children's questions

INTERACTION WITH PARENTS

Casual, chatty, personal	Warm yet professional	Avoidance, cold, abrupt

CONSCIOUSNESS IN RELATION TO TIME

Seems unaware of time, lets each activity continue until there is a rush at end of morning	Allows morning to flow without rush, but on time	Constantly checking watch, abrupt transitions

These triads, or polarities with middle ground, are intended to lend mobility to the process of observation. They are not meant as a checklist, which would defeat the purpose. This approach to observation is beautifully described in the following quotation from *Howard's End* by E. M. Forster:

> The business man who assumes that this life is everything, and the mystic who asserts that it is nothing, fail, on this side and on that, to hit the truth. "Yes, I see, dear; it's about halfway between," Aunt Juley had hazarded in earlier years. No; truth, being alive, was not halfway between anything. It was only to be found by continuous excursions into either realm, and though proportion is the final secret, to espouse it at the outset is to ensure sterility.

In closing, a further question the mentor may ask herself after the observation is, "What did I not see that I would have expected to see? Was there something missing in the morning's experience?" This question may help to bring the morning's observations into focus and provide additional insights for the mentoring conversation that will follow.

5. The Art of Fruitful Conversation

Carol Nasr Griset and Kim Raymond

"What is more splendid than gold?" "Light."
"What is more refreshing than light?" "Conversation."

> —Goethe, The Green Snake and the Beautiful Lily

When we think of conversation, we tend to focus on what is said. On further reflection, however, we realize that listening is just as essential a part of conversation as speaking. A true conversation is a meeting of two individuals who together have the possibility of seeing something new arise from their understanding of one another.

The Role of Listening

When I am listened to, it creates me.

> —Brenda Ueland, Tell Me More

At the center of the mentoring relationship is the encounter we might call the mentoring conversation. This conversation most often takes place after the morning visit when the children have either gone home or into the aftercare program. At the heart of the mentoring conversation is the art of listening. Why is listening the mentor's primary responsibility? How does listening contribute to an individual's creative process? What do I have to do in order to truly listen to another?

> *The way we listen enables others to speak. In other words, to actively listen means giving others the possibility of saying things that they could not otherwise have said—or could not have said in the same way.*
>
> —Heinz Zimmermann (1996)

Active listening to another is an act of love. It is a spiritual deed and requires courage, self-discipline and practice. Through listening, a mentor makes themself available as a guide in the self-development process of the other. As listening mentors, we strive to create a fertile space within ourselves where the other's words may take root and grow. We open ourselves to them so that their unique way of being in the world and of caring for young children may flourish. We create a space for them to feel whole, valued, and understood.

> *Listen to the new teacher. Listening is perhaps the most important thing you can do. Let the new teacher tell her story and encourage her in the telling. This is the story of preparation, questions, new ideas, struggles, concerns, worries. Be genuinely interested and try to resist the urge to tell her how you handled those problems or the temptation to sort it all out for her. And when you listen, listen; don't take notes.*
>
> —*Trevor Mepham*

Trust in the mentor will make it safe for the mentee to speak honestly. According to one experienced mentor, it is crucial that the mentor not have a "hidden agenda" in the conversation, such as wanting to bring attention to a specific defect or issue that one thinks is causing difficulties. The mentor's attitude needs to be one of interest, and of not knowing what the other wants, feels or thinks. The mentor cannot assume or presume what the other will bring. This atmosphere of openness allows the mentee to be vulnerable in their feelings and creative in their thinking as they speak. In turn, the mentor may hear something profound that they needed to hear at that moment from the person being mentored.

> *If we concentrate our hearing until we are filled with the sound of another's voice, then an intimate encounter with the essence of the speaker can come about.*
>
> —*Heinz Zimmermann (1996)*

Attentive listening means we consciously work to withhold judgment and comparison. We withhold our responses, our thoughts, and our expectations. In this process of holding back, we make space for the other and thus become truly available to them. We become aware that another's approach, though different from our own, does not necessarily need to be corrected or changed. When asked what would be helpful from a mentor, a new teacher said, "Before you make a judgment, ask us, 'Why did you do it that way?' Even though you may be more experienced, please remain open to our new ideas."

> *In committing ourselves to listen, we have a chance to dissolve old forms and prejudgments, to loosen ourselves from our thinking and acquire a different kind of knowing—that which comes through our feeling and willing—our impressionable receptivity.*
>
> —*Georg Kühlewind (2004)*

In "Self-Education as the Basis for the Art of Mentoring" (chapter 1), Andrea discusses how mentors need to "forget" what they know in the interests of serving the growth of the mentee.

Before entering the classroom of our mentee, we allow our carefully built up concepts of "how things are done" to dissolve, so that the possibility is created for something altogether new to appear.

The mentor listens with all of the senses. With the ears, they hear the words and tone of voice. With the eyes, they perceive the other person's eyes, facial expressions, body language, and gesture.

If we listen to another person as though to a piece of music, we will get to know their "composing style" and give them space to express this style freely. Through deep, empathic listening, the mentor becomes aware of the mentee's vision and striving. The quality of the mentor's listening will draw out and confirm what the mentee already knows. The mentor observes and listens to ascertain the purposefulness in the mentee's decisions and actions. They may be able to encourage a gift in the mentee that the mentee may not fully appreciate in themself. For example, in listening to the mentee tell a story to the children, the mentor may see through an awkward presentation of the story to experience the mentee's enthusiasm and real gift for creating imaginative pictures in storytelling.

Keen listening will allow the mentor to ascertain if the mentee is speaking out of their own understanding, or is borrowing from someone else. Perhaps the mentee is expressing what they think the mentor wants to hear; perhaps they are saying what they think they "should" be saying as a new teacher, or what they have heard other teachers say. With sensitive questions and empathy, the mentor can guide the mentee toward authenticity, self-confidence, and true creativity.

The Role of Speaking

Improving our ability to converse means improving our ability to interact socially. We can give our partners-in-conversation opportunities to develop themselves, arrive at insights, find solutions and feel supported, or we can use conversation solely to develop and validate ourselves.

—*Heinz Zimmermann (1996)*

With this in mind, a mentor's listening will inform their speaking. Through open and fully attentive listening our speaking will arise naturally, as we seek to clarify what the mentee is saying. Our thoughtful questions will support the mentee in discovering their capacities and developing themself as a teacher.

In moving from listening to speaking, asking questions is most helpful when the questions serve to develop the themes brought forth by the mentee. Bringing an attitude of warmth and empathy to their questions, the mentor seeks to hear more about the mentee's ideas. We may be able to remember how difficult it can be for a new teacher to express intentions and impressions to a seasoned teacher.

Remember not to patronize. The new teacher is intelligent, skilled, inventive, sensitive, and she may have something to teach you. Draw ideas and possibilities out of her through questions and observations and don't give easy answers. Have the tact to let her discover her own answers.

—*Trevor Mepham*

As mentors, we may need to remind ourselves that in order to understand another, we "stand under" them with a respectful and learning attitude, remembering that it takes years of teaching to discover one's own style and learn to be comfortably oneself with the children.

> *Before I go into a teacher's classroom, I first remind myself to look for something which that teacher can do better than I. What can I find to truly admire in the other adult?*
>
> —Else Gottgens, long-time mentor

Establishing a Relationship and Asking Helpful Questions

Building a relationship with the mentee is a prerequisite for having a fruitful conversation. Early in the mentoring process, the mentor will need to ask the mentee, "What do you want, hope for, and expect from the mentoring relationship?" We can then clarify, if necessary, how we see our role as a mentor. (For specific suggestions about gathering demographic and other practical information from the mentee, please see chapter 2.)

Both mentor and mentee will find it helpful for the mentee to complete a self-assessment before the visit. This should include self-perceived areas of strength and weakness, and any concerns the mentee has about their work. When asking the mentee to prepare such a self-assessment prior to the visit, the mentor may help the process by asking the mentee to consider the following:

"What part of your work gives you the most joy and satisfaction?"

"What do you find especially difficult?"

"What are your priorities for this year?"

An experienced mentor suggested that if something is hard for the mentee, the mentor can encourage them to narrow down the area of difficulty. For example, if the mentee is challenged by circle time, the mentor may help pinpoint the challenge. The mentor can begin by asking what parts of the circle go smoothly. From an awareness of the mentee's strengths, the mentor can better help them approach the problem.

It is important to ask open questions that encourage the mentee to become more conscious of what they already know. A mentee is likely to appreciate questions that focus their awareness. During the mentoring visit, such open questions might include: "What do you think are your strengths?"; "In what ways have you grown since you started working with young children?" In helping a mentee to clarify communication with us, we may offer a comment such as, "Let me see if I understand what you are saying." Then the mentor may reflect back as clearly as possible what they have heard. Clarity will enable the mentor to validate and support what the mentee is expressing.

In helping the mentee to reflect on the day, the mentor may find questions such as the following useful: "How was the morning for you?"; "What parts of it do you think went well?"; "What parts of the morning were most challenging?" In supporting and respecting the growth of the mentee, a mentor might need to guide them away from labeling or blaming a child or parent in a difficult situation A mentor may be able to offer a new approach that focuses the mentee on what positive actions they might initiate to help resolve a difficulty. The mentor can help the mentee to expand on self-observation by asking questions such as:

"Can you tell me more about that?"

"Can you think of any way you might be contributing to the problem?"

"Have you thought about a possible plan of action?"

By asking the mentee to describe the areas where they feel most competent, the mentor acknowledges the mentee's abilities and reminds them of why they have chosen this work as their vocation. In addition, by allowing the mentee to talk about their challenges, the mentor creates the opportunity for the mentee to place their pride, vulnerability, or embarrassment into the chalice of conversation.

Additional Aspects of Conversation

There is another kind of conversation to pay attention to during the mentoring visit: the daily exchanges the mentee has while working. How is the conversation between teacher and children; the conversation/relationship between teacher and assistant; and the conversation/relationship between the teacher and the parents? Are the children being heard and are the children hearing the teacher? The mentor will be looking for the quality of these "conversations" even though they may sometimes be nonverbal. Is it a fruitful exchange, and is there understanding? Does the assistant feel acknowledged; do the parents feel appreciated? What is the quality of the exchanges between the mentee and the people they relate to every day?

A mentor may be asked for help with the mentee's relationship with the parents of the children in the class. They may suggest that the mentee approach the teacher-parent relationship as one would approach a conversation: that is, by setting aside pre-judgments and expectations and offering an open and empathic atmosphere for an exchange to take place. The mentor may remind the mentee of the importance of fully attentive listening when interacting with parents, so as to experience with them, as with the children, the love that grows out of interest. The mentee may need to be encouraged in embracing and respecting the parents' central role in their child's life. It can come as a surprise to a beginning teacher how much of their work will be with parents. Mentors can have an important role to play in helping new teachers find ways to include parents in the life of the class. Occasionally, the mentor may be asked to help the mentee plan a parent evening. By active listening and reflective feedback, a mentor can encourage the mentee's enthusiasm and help focus their plans for sharing their ideas and observations with the parents. The mentor's experienced perspective is valuable in this area and can serve as a reminder to the mentee about how much there is to be learned from the parents.

Sometimes a mentor may enter into a mentoring relationship with an experienced teacher who is resistant to feedback or deeply entrenched in particular patterns or habits of relating to young children. The mentor may then approach more deeply the intention behind the teacher's actions, asking, "What is the thought behind the action?" They may pose the question to the teacher, "What are your reasons for doing it this way?" "Is it having the effect you hoped for?" "Have you ever considered trying. . . ?"

Occasionally, a mentor will encounter a mentee who is wondering whether to pursue teaching as a career; or the mentor might have this question. It might be helpful to inquire about the mentee's biography and why they chose to enter the field of teaching. The mentor may help the mentee perceive if they are experiencing a temporary difficulty or whether a bigger question exists. This situation calls for honesty and tact from the mentor. A question such as, "Does teaching nourish you as a life's work?" may be helpful.

Some Practical Considerations

Just as the children's activity is nourished by a healthy environment, the mentoring conversation is affected by surrounding circumstances. Is the setting private? Is it quiet enough to allow for focus and concentration? What time of day is it? Are the participants hungry, tired, or needing a break? In some teacher education programs, it is the mentee's responsibility to ensure that the conversation is given the necessary respect within the framework of the day so that a fruitful exchange can take place. In this case, the mentee will be expected to attend to the practical details of arranging an appropriate setting as well as allowing for adequate time. For example, the mentee might need to schedule a substitute to cover for them if they have afternoon faculty duties. One mentor noted the difficulty of conducting a mentoring conversation while sitting at a picnic table on a windy winter afternoon during the mentee's playground duty.

Sometimes, the planning may be the responsibility of the mentor. The mentor will be prepared to ask the mentee to "make time" for the conversation during the school day. Eating lunch together after a morning observation may help the transition into a more relaxed conversation. Ideally, there would be some time between the observation and the conversation to allow both to collect their thoughts and digest the morning's experiences.

If the mentee has an assistant, or is an assistant, meeting for half an hour with both individuals before meeting alone with the mentee can be helpful. In this way, the mentor has an opportunity to ask how the morning went for each of them, separately and as a team. By creating an atmosphere of trust and empathy, the mentor gives each a chance to speak openly about working together. If there are struggles between the two, the mentor can normalize or provide neutral ground to the struggles between teacher and assistant, likening them to the struggles in any close relationship. They may need to affirm how important it is for the children to experience an atmosphere of respect and caring between the two. The mentor may need to help the pair to have realistic expectations of one another and of their relationship.

It often helps to put a mentee at ease if mentor and mentee are able to socialize outside of the mentoring conversation. They may have a meal together or take a walk, or the mentor may stay at the mentee's house. The casual time that mentor and mentee spend together outside of the classroom in an informal setting may lead to expanded or enhanced conversation and deeper understanding of one another. If the mentor stays at the home of the mentee, they may have the opportunity to meet the mentee's spouse or family and gain a greater awareness of the mentee's life situation. This broader perspective will allow the mentor to offer a greater depth of support, compassion, and encouragement.

The passage of time is a mysterious element in the mentoring relationship. The quality of conversation will change as mentor and mentee come to know one another. As trust develops, conversations will ripen and yield more insight. Another aspect of time the mentor may notice is that, often, it will not be until the next day or the next week that the significance of a question or comment will surface. The mentor may find an opportunity to mention these insights or ask additional questions in a follow-up phone conversation, email, or visit.

Qualities to Cultivate; Additional Thoughts

Through the ages, people have sought wise counsel from those who are more experienced. As a listener, a guide, and a mirror, our role as mentor is profound. Foremost for the mentor is facility in the art of communication. As experienced teachers, we come to the mentoring role with a wide variety of skills and an abundance of gifts to share. In order to be truly effective in aiding the self-development of the other, we have a responsibility to hone our communication skills through workshops and study (see chapter 1).

Often a mentor can spend much time and energy in conversation with a mentee and wonder if there was a positive effect. It may be helpful for the mentor to create a way for the mentee to give feedback regarding the mentoring experience. Such feedback could be sent to the mentor and/or initiating body. This information could provide valuable insights for the mentor's self-evaluation and bring to light aspects of the mentor's listening and speaking that need more awareness.

It is worthwhile for the mentor to review the balance of listening and speaking after a conversation, and to ask themself about the quality of connection—"How was the understanding between us?" As mentors, we need to develop the self-knowledge that informs us as to whether we should learn to listen more or to speak more. What is our natural tendency and how do we cultivate the other capacity? A mentor must be able to practice reflection on their own motives, strengths, and weaknesses, asking, for example, "How do I respond to criticism or praise?" Our ability to be helpful as a mentor is grounded in who we are and who we are striving to become. If we remain open to the possibilities for growth, mentoring has the possibility of transforming the mentor as well as the mentee.

This chapter began with the quotation from Brenda Ueland:

When I am listened to, it creates me.

As mentors, let us strive to cultivate the capacity to listen in a way that makes this thought a reality.

6. Pearls of Wisdom: The Role of Advice in Mentoring

Nancy Foster

The mentoring relationship offers a golden opportunity for mutual growth and learning, and a forum for collegial exploration of questions about pedagogy and human relations. As one mentor asked somewhat plaintively, however, "Is it ever appropriate to offer our 'pearls of wisdom?'"

It is important that a mentor be a good listener, and that they enter the mentoring situation with openness and a readiness to support the mentee's goals rather than impose their own preconceived ideas. On the other hand, there also exist certain essential qualities of Waldorf early childhood education, as described in chapter 3. Isn't it important that the mentor carry a commitment to these essentials into the mentoring relationship, and bring them to the mentee's attention if the mentor feels something is lacking? And what if the mentee is asking for advice: "What should I do to make snack time more peaceful?" Is it wrong for the mentor to offer a tried-and-true approach, developed from experience? After all, a teacher or caregiver becomes a mentor when they have developed skills and capacities from their years with young children and parents, from study, and from inner work arising from anthroposophy. They are, to be sure, still actively engaged in a path of continuing development; but they are also something more than simply a peer of the mentee.

Is there a way to acknowledge the mentor's greater experience without creating a situation of hierarchy—without an implied judgment of the worth of either person's potential as a teacher or caregiver and as a human being? Can a mentor offer advice in a way that still leaves the mentee free to find their own path?

Possibilities—Not Rules

Years ago, our school arranged for several European master teachers to visit us, one each year, to offer an intensive course on early childhood, to visit our classrooms, and to meet with us. These teachers brought a wealth of knowledge and experience. I remember that after their visits, we always noticed that our classrooms became somewhat chaotic and unsettled. We soon realized that this chaos reflected our own inner condition; our work with these master teachers had brought new and stimulating ideas, and we were questioning many of our classroom practices. Of course, the children sensed this off-balance condition and reacted as children usually do. Understanding the cause, we were able to take this in stride, and soon, order was restored as we worked through our questions inwardly.

We were grateful for this experience with a variety of master teachers. We perceived that each teacher was deeply rooted in anthroposophy and the understanding of the young child; yet they had arrived at quite different practices in classroom work, from the rhythm of the day to festival life to the details of watercolor painting or rest time. This was an invaluable perspective for us—the realization that in Waldorf education there can be no "one right way," but that each of us must strive to deepen our connection to the source of Waldorf education, to learn from those with experience as well as from each other, to question, and gradually to find our own way. This perspective can help to illuminate the question of advice-giving in the mentoring relationship.

The answer to the question, "Is it ever appropriate to offer our 'pearls of wisdom?'" must be, "It depends." It depends in part on the spirit in which these pearls are offered. Can the mentor find a way to give advice that does not proclaim rules, but rather opens possibilities for another approach to a situation or suggests a new way of thinking about a question? Can the mentor describe their own way or point of view, at the same time sharing reasons and mentioning alternative ways? Such advice will support the mentee in taking another step in development, while respecting their need to explore a question and ultimately make their own decisions.

Those master teachers who visited our school did not hesitate to give advice or to tell us how they did things. However, they always gave this advice or information in the context of the reasons for their approach. Invariably they would say, "This is how I do it, but of course there are other ways too," or words to that effect. (Of course, it was sometimes clear that they wondered how anyone could possibly want to do it one of those other ways!—but their intent was clear. They wished to leave us free to think the matter through.) Often, they would ask a teacher they had observed, "Why did you do it that way?" If the teacher had a good reason, that was all-important. This approach to giving advice is, obviously, quite different from saying, "Rest time has to come before circle time;" or "never give children only one color to paint with," or "you should always cover the windows with drapes."

Anchors in a Sea of Uncertainties

A very different—almost a polar—relationship to advice was demonstrated by another visiting teacher, a warm and positive person, who met with our faculty to discuss a particular element of the weekly rhythm. Wanting to avoid any appearance of authority and to leave us free to find our own way, she warded off all our attempts to ascertain what she thought or how she approached the work with the children, instead asking us, "What do you think? How do you do it?" This was extremely frustrating! We were interested in her ideas, and wanted her to trust that we would be able to think about them and reach our own conclusions. A mentor who never gives advice or takes a position on an issue could be equally frustrating to a mentee, leaving them to flounder without a sense of direction.

The answer to the question about whether to offer advice also depends on the particular situation and the particular mentor/mentee relationship. If the mentee is a new teacher or caregiver, for instance, and is experiencing many challenges, they may need more specific advice as a sort of "first aid" while learning to find their way. A limited number of firm suggestions may serve as anchors in a sea of uncertainties. There will be time in future years for them to work through their own ways. A more experienced person, or a former assistant who has moved into a lead position, on the other hand, is at a different stage in professional growth. They may benefit more if the mentor spends time helping to clarify their questions and sharpen their observations of their own work and its results.

Some mentees present the mentor with many specific questions, perhaps involving individual children they find challenging. Such a mentee may want "recipes for success," possibly feeling insecure or wishing to avoid looking at underlying, more deep-seated causes for the challenges they are encountering. In such situations, the mentor may be tempted to fall into a question-and-answer mode. The "recipe" approach, however, is full of pitfalls. A recipe-seeking mentee may attempt to apply a piece of advice to every situation that appears similar, failing to realize that the essential factor is the particular child or group of children, along with the particular teacher. Thus, a mentor who is confronted with this kind of questioning will probably wish to find a way to help the mentee find their own answers. Such an effort will not provide a "quick fix," but will in the end be of more help to the mentee.

Tact and Discernment

In contrast, some mentees seem to resist any sort of advice, always seeking to justify their own way or offering reasons why the advice would not work. This is sometimes the case even when the mentee seems to be asking for help. In such a situation, it may be possible through conversation (see chapter 5) for the mentor to get to know the mentee better and come to understand how best to offer needed help and support. "Ask, don't tell," was the rule of thumb of one experienced teacher educator I know. Tactful but persistent questions may help the mentee to see what is needed. In some cases, a sharing of perceptions of the mentor/mentee relationship may be worthwhile. The mentor may say, "It seems as if you might prefer that I not offer specific advice. Is that the case? What would be more helpful?" The mentee may not be conscious of their resistance, and such an observation and question may bring this to light and allow them to share their needs and perceptions more fully with the mentor.

A mentoring situation where the mentee is in a non-Waldorf setting requires special tact on the part of the mentor. It would be very discouraging for such a mentee to be made to feel there is only one right way to do things. This circumstance can provide a wonderful opportunity for the mentor and mentee to explore together the essential qualities of Waldorf education and try to see how these can be approached in a setting that necessarily limits the possibilities. This can be a challenge and a learning experience for the mentor as well as the mentee.

In conclusion, we might answer the opening question, "Is it ever appropriate to offer our 'pearls of wisdom?'" by saying, "Giving advice can be a good thing, if . . . ." And we might complete the sentence with the following considerations: (a) if the mentor has first tried to discern the real question or need; (b) if the advice is offered with humility; (c) if the advice arises not from a recipe or dogma but from taking the actual circumstances into account; (d) if reasons for the advice are shared; (e) if a context of other possible approaches and their pros and cons is given; and (f) if the mentor offers the advice in such a way that the mentee is given space and time to consider and work with the idea, leaving them free both inwardly and outwardly to find their own way.

7. *Accountability: Written Records*

Nancy Foster

A record of a mentoring visit goes to the mentee and to the initiating body, which may be an early childhood education program, a school committee, or a pedagogical coordinator. However, there is some disagreement (see chapter 11) about whether the record of the visit should be only between the mentor and the mentee. The written record of a mentoring visit serves at least three purposes.

- The record is primarily for the benefit of the mentee. It provides an objective view of their current work, support and encouragement in their striving, and a mirror of their questions. It may also include "homework" for the next observation, as well as specific suggestions for the work.

- For the mentor, writing the record allows time for reflection, for review of the mentoring conversation, and for working with the sleep process to reach a perspective of warm objectivity, so as to offer the mentee both support and suggestions for further development.

- For the director of a training program, or for a school committee, the record offers an account of the visit and a picture of the mentor's perception of the mentee's work and development.

An early childhood education program or a school may provide a recording form with specific points for observation and comment; or it may give broader guidelines for a narrative record. In essence, the written record is a summary or overview of what was discussed in the conversation of mentor and mentee following the classroom visit. In most cases, the mentoring conversation and the record might include the following components.

- A brief description of the classroom setting and demographics of the class

- A description of the mentee's responsibilities in the class and how they carry forth these responsibilities

- Areas of strength and capability observed

- Areas where further development is suggested

- Particular questions or concerns carried by the mentee

- "Homework" suggested by the mentor: a goal to be met, a new approach to be tried in a particular aspect of the work, an inner exercise, a child observation, etc. A valuable role of the mentor's visit, which can be reflected in the report, is to leave the mentee with a question that will stimulate and support their development, both personally and professionally.

It will be worthwhile for the mentor to notice whether they and the mentee are seeing the same things in the mentee's work. That is, are the mentee's questions and concerns in accord with what the mentor observes as areas of greatest need? If not, the mentor may ask questions and offer observations during the conversation in order to bring more awareness to the mentee. The mentor will also want to listen carefully to the mentee's concerns and take them seriously. Detailed consideration of the mentoring conversation is found in chapter 5.

Two aspects of a teacher's or caregiver's work that are of paramount importance, but may be difficult for a mentor to observe, are work with colleagues and work with parents. Some indications may surface in the course of conversations or interactions, in which case these may be discussed and mentioned in the record.

It can be a valuable support to the mentee's professional development if they are asked to take some notes during the mentor/mentee conversation and then to write an account of the mentor's comments, questions, and suggestions. This requires an active involvement of the mentee's will forces in the process of digesting and putting into writing what they have heard. The mentee's account would then be sent to the mentor soon after the visit; the mentor could add to the report as needed to clarify points or fill in any missing thoughts, returning the final version to the mentee as well as sending a copy to the initiating body if this is part of the process.

Alternatively, the mentee can be asked not to take notes, but to listen deeply to what the mentor has to say and to engage in conversation. All this information and the resulting conversation would then be reflected in the mentor's notes that will follow.

When the mentor writes the record of the visit, a copy should be sent to the mentee, who then has a chance to confirm that the record gives an accurate overview of the mentoring conversation. Since all substantive aspects of the mentoring observation should have been addressed in the conversation, the record should not include observations or concerns that the mentor and mentee have not already discussed. The mentor and mentee should, however, make sure that the record expresses the perceptions of both parties. Again, the final version should be sent to both the mentee and the initiating body.

In either case—whether the initial report is written by the mentor or the mentee—both mentor and mentee will contribute to the final record that goes to the pedagogical or program director, or school committee.

For an early childhood education program, it is important that the mentoring record be kept confidential. It is not intended for the school where the mentee is teaching, though the mentee is free to share it if they wish. The mentor is responsible only to the mentee and the training program, not to the mentee's school. In the event, however, that the mentoring visit has been initiated by a school, the mentor is responsible to the school as outlined in chapter 2 in the section "Clarity of Expectations."

It is important to bear in mind that a mentoring record is not an evaluation (see chapter 11). The record is, rather, an account of a conversation that has taken place between a mentor and mentee—a conversation with the purpose of fostering the mentee's personal and professional growth.

8. Meeting at the Eye of the Needle: Mentoring on the Path of Adult Learning

Susan Silverio

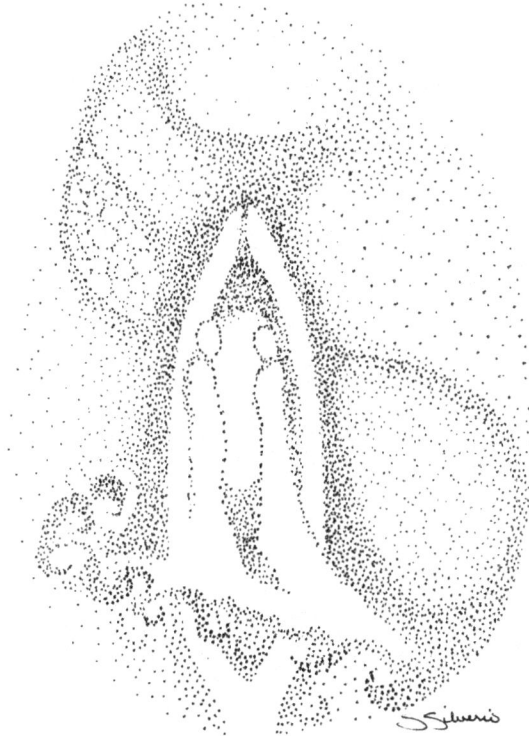

And so they meet—two early childhood teachers or caregivers.

Perhaps one is retired from classroom teaching.

Perhaps one has just begun their first Waldorf kindergarten class, or a home-based LifeWays center. Or perhaps both are seasoned teachers seeking further development and the inspiration to continue.

Both are united on behalf of the young child and the future of human development.

At this time, one is called to serve as a mentor.

We will call the other the "mentee" for now.

Although one is designated the mentor, both are on a path of self-education and adult learning. What are the various paths of adult learning, and what are the processes involved?

And how might these relate to mentoring?

In *Awakening the Will: Principles and Processes of Adult Learning*, author Coenraad van Houten describes three learning paths. One is learning for life, in a scheduled course of study and training, imparted by teachers, often in institutes and schools organized for higher education. The second path is learning through life. "Everyone is constantly faced with a discrepancy between their inner faculties, strengths and weaknesses, on the one hand, and what comes towards them as necessities, questions, and challenges of life, on the other. This is the situation of Destiny Learning." The third path is learning to live in the reality of the spiritual world. Rudolf Steiner illuminates this path: the modern path of self-knowledge. He points out that instruction and counsel are helpful, but the task is to find our Teacher within. In van Houten's words, "The highest learning objective that exists is: to become ever more a human being, to be able to experience our true being in the cosmic worlds of our origin. This is so we can become better able to fulfill our tasks here on earth."

It is the adult ego that integrates these three learning paths. All three paths work together as the adult develops the lively art of nourishing the young child's unfolding will forces in the work and play of daily life through the seasons. As Steiner-based education cares for the entire human being—body, soul and spirit—early childhood is recognized as a time when the incarnating soul and spirit are taking up residence in the earthly form, surrounding the physical body with a cloud of life forces and recreating it in order to take up the individuality's life purpose. The being of the child is completely open to their surroundings, including the thoughts and feelings of the adults who relate to them. The child devotes themself to absorbing all they encounter. It is essential, therefore, that the adult is protective of the young child's life forces and is striving to be worthy of the young child's imitation. This includes harmonizing our thoughts and feelings as well as our speech and movement. If we are honest, we recognize this work as a lifelong path of learning and development.

Becoming a mentor is also a process of learning as the mentor moves from their own experience and their own incarnating of the essentials of Waldorf education to meet the mentee, who is moving into the future on their own path of study, life experience, and inner work.

So, perhaps, it would be worthwhile to reflect on exactly what the processes of adult learning might be. We know that the young child learns through imitation—through empathy with their environment and the actions and inner qualities of the teacher; the grade-school child's life of feeling is being carried and developed through the "beloved authority" of the teacher; and the high school or college student works with ideas, still seeking the star of the individual self.

The adult learner, however, is now able to call upon their own Spirit Self to navigate into life, to consciously direct and integrate experience into knowledge and capacities. At the age of twenty-one, the very life forces that we strive to protect in early childhood are freed for self-education.

Coenraad van Houten works with the seven processes of adult learning, based on the seven processes of life described by Rudolf Steiner in the 1916 lecture *The Riddle of Humanity* (1990), in explaining all of biological life, including human life processes and perception. On a biological level these seven processes are: (1) breathing, (2) warming, (3) digesting, (4) eliminating/absorbing, (5) maintaining, (6) growing, and (7) reproducing. The first three processes involve taking something in from outside as physical nourishment (air, warmth, and food). The fourth process is the turning point of transforming these substances internally. The last three processes involve bringing forth something from within (sustaining the body, growing, and giving birth).

"Adult Learning is based on the use our ego makes of the life processes that were originally involved in the forming of our body. Our available etheric forces, energized by the ego, produce Adult Learning" (van Houten, 43). The seven natural life processes become available to the adult as the seven learning processes: (1) perceiving, (2) relating, (3) digesting, (4) individualizing, (5) practicing, (6) growing faculties, and (7) creating something new.

The first process, perceiving, is observing the world through the senses. There is a breathing quality, in that something is taken in, internalized, and needs to be breathed out as well. Outer sense impressions do not simply stream into the adult, as is the case with the young child. An adult must be attentive. Only then does one hear a speaker, read a book, perceive a sound, color, movement, and so on.

The second process, relating, requires a person to form a connection with what has been observed. An inner activity of interest is required to warm up (or cool down if need be) what has been perceived. For example, a monotone presentation would require a listener to consciously engage the ego in order to discover the essentials being presented. The individual ego would also need to be engaged in order not to be carried away by a fiery speaker.

The third process, digesting, is to assimilate what has been taken in. Just as food must be completely broken down in order to be digested by the physical organism, so also adults must digest what has been seen and heard before it can provide spiritual nourishment.

The fourth process, individualizing, is the central and crucial process of the seven. This is the internal turning point where there is a sorting out of that which the individual may transform for his own use, and that which must be eliminated. This is the "aha!" moment of adult learning, when something is experienced as new, as if born from within and truly one's own. In order for this to occur, there needs to be time and space for this transformation to happen freely. This process can only take place if the ego has been active in working with the first three processes of observing, relating and digesting. Someone whose ego does not take up and work with material may continue to "do their own thing." This would be individualism—remaining in old habits and attitudes or acting merely out of personal preference. On the other hand, someone could take up new material and adhere to it blindly, without working it through with their own ego, neglecting the step of digesting. This could lead to a kind of rigid dogmatism. These polarities are balanced only when the adult ego is engaged in all of these learning processes.

Once a new insight or impulse is gained, the final learning stages are practicing, growing new faculties, and creating something new. The fifth process, practicing, allows what has been realized to take root. There may not necessarily be a feeling of immediate success. One needs to have the courage and perseverance to practice what is being learned and to find a way to practice that renews vitality.

In the sixth process, growing new faculties, all of the preceding work needs to "go to sleep" so that it can reawaken as an inner capacity.

Finally, there is the possibility of the seventh process of creating something new, something more than the sum of the parts.

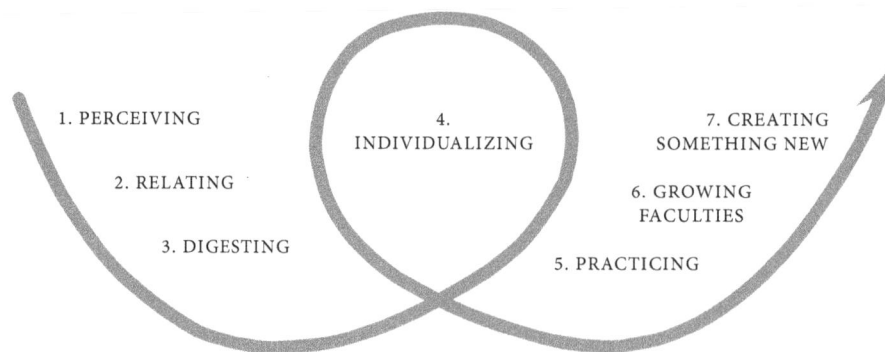

An overview of the seven life processes (van Houten, 53). Used with author's permission.

This sequence of seven processes describes something more than the acquiring of a skill or a method of teaching. It describes, rather, the development of new capacities. For truly human development, the middle step of individualizing is essential.

An example of this learning sequence would be a beginning teacher who works out of imitation of another teacher. As they enter their second year of teaching, they may have a dawning realization that there isn't necessarily one "Our School" way that requires that a child's birthday be celebrated in a specific manner. The new teacher had assumed that what their colleague described was what every teacher did. The new teacher's mentor assures them that it was fine to do things, in the first year, just as the fellow teacher described. Gradually, the new teacher develops the feeling that this way doesn't feel quite right; they begin questioning, trying to discern what fits, and so on. Finally, the new teacher begins to find and clarify their own way. This is never a finished product, rather, always a process of development, but now arising out of the teacher's Self rather than imitation.

It is valuable for a mentor to acknowledge the gifts as well as the challenges of the mentee. Strengths may be cultivated while challenging areas may be developed more slowly over the course of time. For example, a teacher may rely on their natural storytelling ability, while taking a number of years to explore puppetry and to learn to sing in a way that nourishes the young child.

This sequence may take a shorter or a longer time for an individual teacher, and some areas will proceed at different paces than others. The experience of individualizing can sometimes be precipitated by contact with a self-realized person who exemplifies the last three stages of practicing, growth, and creativity. The teacher may then discover that it is not so much what is done, but how it is done.

Although the processes of learning are sequential, they are also simultaneous. A mentor may meet a mentee in any of these processes and offer encouragement to continue to explore, to study, to deepen, to make the work one's own, and to practice, express, and create.

This is a challenging path, and resistance can easily develop on the level of either thinking, feeling, or willing. Van Houten offers the following approaches. If we encounter resistance on the thinking level, it can be met with interest and objective observation. If there seems to be resistance on the level of feeling, we can practice deep listening. If fear seems to be offering resistance to the life of willing, movement may be encouraged through artistic activity.

Resistance may originate at an unconscious level out of past experiences, temperament, or hidden antipathy toward the mentor. Resistance may also be seen as an indication of a question that wants to be asked. A mentee may be able to articulate a question if a mentor can foster an open and inquiring manner. Some mentees may have a desire for the direction of an authority, while others may resist or resent any kind of suggestion. Even while the mentor may hold deeply the essential ideals of Waldorf education (and perhaps the principles and practices of LifeWays Care or RIE as well), they need to recognize that even these must be temporarily set aside in meeting another who is in the process of adult learning. Instead of giving directives and advice, a mentor may come to meet a mentee as they stand at the eye of the needle by asking a question such as, "What are you working on now?" The question may engage the ego of the mentee, and stimulate quiet contemplation.

"Human beings really are aware of much more than they know about in their daytime consciousness. Their higher beings know, their conscience knows. In their subconscious soul-regions a large amount of wisdom is stored" (van Houten, 60). From these recesses, something of a breakthrough may occur. What we know becomes understanding or a new way of sensing. Very often, this process of individualizing sets off a will impulse. An understanding becomes an intention or decision. This process is encouraged and reinforced when a mentor works with questions instead of answers.

It may be helpful for the mentee to work on one thing at a time. A mentor can offer encouragement along this challenging path of learning as an adult by sharing their own questions, challenges, and joys as appropriate.

A mentee may have questions to pose to a mentor as well. Experienced mentors have relayed that these questions have been an opportunity to bring to consciousness and to articulate their own intentions and understandings. Such questions may even prompt changes in the mentor's own practice.

Truly, the process of adult learning, as a mentor as well as a mentee, can be a lifelong path of learning and development. To consciously choose to remain active in this process of learning takes courage, but engenders life and brings one closer to the realm of the young child.

9. *"Tell Me More":*
Opening to the Mentoring Process

Anna Rainville

When I was first asked to be a mentor for a new teacher, I was eager to be the one with experience to rescue a difficult situation. Any success from this first encounter was short term. I failed to grasp the whole picture or see the fine details because I judged the situation with some fixed ideas about this role.

When, soon after, I discovered the origin of the word mentor as I was teaching the Odyssey in the tenth grade, I began to understand the profound implications.

Homer tells how Odysseus asks his friend Mentor to watch over his young son, Telemachus, when Odysseus leaves for the Trojan War. Mentor's guidance continues until the boy comes of age.

Athena, the goddess of wisdom, disguises herself as Mentor and accompanies Telemachus on an important journey, acting as a witness and an affirming presence to the arduous task of the young man's self-discovery.

Later, I discovered more fully the mythical roots of being a mentor as described by Norman Fischer, a Zen priest.

> Any process of deep or lasting growth involves mentors; their effects on us are more mysterious and far-reaching than the practical aid or advice they provide. We learn from books, we learn from our senses, our thoughts, our emotions, our doing. We learn from what others tell us and from what we overhear. Though mentoring may include several of these modes of learning, it is essentially different, because the mentor's simple presence in our lives creates an alchemy that transfers a subtle inner power. This transference cannot happen in any other way (Fischer 2011).

Several wise elders have modeled professional and personal integrity for me. Justine Forbes, in her elegant nineties at the time of this writing, treated me, even as an adolescent, as if I mattered. For almost sixty years, I have turned to her as an example of how to be a mother, a daughter, a partner, and a teacher. She listens more than speaks, shows interest and amusement at my many predicaments, and makes me feel seen and heard. Her questions are challenging, probing, revealing, and never judgmental. The way she listens opens a door to an answer or clarity I never knew was within me. I feel that when I am with her, we can be timeless and free.

I especially owe my love for Waldorf education to Lydia Lecraw, who taught at the Waldorf Institute in Garden City, New York. To me, her life exemplified a genuine devotion to goodness, truth, and beauty. Mrs. Lecraw mentored me through the grades by pointing to my own strengths and opening new perspectives for challenging situations, by asking hard questions and then listening without judgment. She often waited for me to ask questions or helped me to formulate them before she offered her own experience and wisdom. Long after she retired from the Waldorf Institute, I visited her each summer in her beautiful hand-built home, in view of Mount Monadnock. Everything about her impressed me: the quality of her voice and rich picture language, the look of wonder on her face when presenting a lesson, her style of dress and posture, her focus and interest in our conversations, her appetite for reading and ideas, her generous community spirit, and her deep commitment to the work of Rudolf Steiner. For me, she personified what an anthroposophist looks like and how they live. As an example of the way she inspired us as teacher trainees, every Advent she transformed her living room into the Göinge Forest from Selma Lagerlöf's *Christmas Rose*, complete with moss and blooming bulbs. We gathered by candlelight to hear her read the story.

I want to honor another treasured mentor, Nancy Mellon, whose eloquence, wit, and wisdom make my life shimmer with possibilities for growth. In her company, I am always learning something! She acts as a fierce editor, a fount of cosmic and mythical knowledge of how the world is connected, a sayer of hard truths, the voice of encouragement, a co-conspirator, a keeper of confidences, a muse, and a friend. I rise in her presence and am grateful.

These days when I am called to be a *mentor*, I realize with wonder that I have over forty years of teaching experience to draw from many dear mentors who continue to inform and inspire my path.

This is what I have been learning:

Giving advice, consulting, coaching, and mentoring all have their special flavors. Some are easily performed by phone, others require in-person meetings. Some are casual, others more formal. Some are temporary and others long-lasting. Some are chosen and others are assigned. To be fruitful, each one depends on mutual trust and honesty.

What makes mentoring different from other supportive relationships? Else Göttgens, the feisty Dutch mentor and author, insisted that to be an effective mentor, one must be present to witness the teacher in action. Without experiencing the teacher in their element, it is difficult to know how to be helpful. Waldorf education develops from the whole to the parts; the same holds true for mentoring. Without experiencing the mentee in their wholeness—in the classroom with the children carrying out the program—the relationship is merely advisory.

Observing in person is ideal, but not always possible. One nervous teacher made me realize that an in-person observation might not be easy or even welcomed. I learned to ask mentees beforehand, "What do you want me to observe or notice (children, transitions, circle, classroom management, and so on)?" This helps me focus and take note of the teacher's concerns.

Even a ten-minute observation can reveal important information. I have learned to always look for the positive and to remind the mentees of their gifts. Once, I met with a teacher who seemed stuck in only one way of perceiving herself—never good enough. She was relieved when I remarked on her comforting gesture with a certain child, her lyrical voice, or the artful way she arranged the indoor garden. This was an opening for further conversations.

I used to arrive with handwork or request the mending basket, so that I could be engaged in a meaningful activity while observing. These days, I bring in my notebook to jot down all the things I want to remember, including: how the children enter, the layout of the room, where is the assistant, how does the teacher move around the room, the way the teacher uses their voice, snippets of conversation between the children, lists of materials in the room, how the light enters, exactly what the teacher says, the sequence of the circle and who is or is not engaged, what happens in transitions, and the rhythm of the day, to name a few. In a column along the side of each page, I write questions that come to mind. If a child asks what I am doing, I say I am writing down all the wonderful things that are happening.

Observation is only the first step. Finding time and space for reflection and the art of conversation follow. Another beloved mentor, Mary Roscoe, always creates a sacred space of simple elegance for our meetings. She sets a beautiful table and makes me feel that our time together is valuable for both of us. There is a vase with flowers, sometimes a gift from nature like a stone or shell depending on the season, a candle, and a cup of tea. We often begin with a verse or a moment of silence to frame what will be shared.

As Waldorf educators, we believe that the power of inquiry commands special meaning when recalling Percival's search for the perfect question to release enchantment. The quality of the conversation and any deep learning come from asking questions that open an unexpected door to understanding something new, to move the mentee further along their professional or personal path. We have a family joke. When my own daughters say in amazement, "Why didn't we know you did this or that?", my answer is "Well, you never asked."

So, I am learning to ask.

In addition to a beautiful setting, initial questions can serve to set a mood of openness and trust. "How are you?" is always a good place to start. "What do you love about teaching?" Gradually, questions can become more focused and sensitive to the mentee's willingness to engage. Norman Fischer writes, in *Sailing Home*, "In addition to our sharing of time, space, and presence with a mentor—[working with a mentor] involves the sharing of stories."

When I am meeting a mentee for the first time, biographical journeys offer rich perspectives. "Tell me how you found your way into Waldorf education or to this school?" Another entry question that serves me well is: "What do I need to know about you to be a good mentor for you?" This handy question can be focused on different situations: "What do I need to know about your child/the school/ the parents, and so on, in order to do my job well?

One of my dear mentors, Jerry Falek, specializes in conversation and deep listening. In one of our first meetings, he stunned me by saying, "Tell me more." From him I am learning ways to set the speaker at ease: "How do you spend your time that's meaningful to you?" and to explore contrasts: "Tell me what brings you joy?" or "What are you working on?"

On the other end of the rainbow, when tears well up, Jerry taught me to ask, "What brings the tears?" and "Stay with the feelings." I have experienced the balm these simple words bring as tenderness and vulnerability emerge. It is remarkable. It confirms for me that our presence, interest, and calm will tell the mentee what they are longing to hear: "I see you. You're safe. You can do this."

Jerry is also a master at speaking in pictures, so necessary to teachers today. I ask a mentee, "Tell me about the picture you are holding for the activity, the morning, the day, the week, the season, the festival, the child, yourself. What does it look like? Tell me more."

I continue to learn how important it is to wait, after a mentee has spoken. In that pause, the longer the better, an answer may arise within them that expresses the heart of the matter.

Sometimes, when a teacher is preoccupied by a child's challenging behavior, I try to redirect the conversation by asking, "What does this child do really well?" and "What does their behavior bring up for you?" I have found that sometimes it is not just about the child, but also the teacher's inner child. The child's behavior stirs the teacher's personal sensitivities. These honest conversations can be a relief and diffuse anxiety.

As educators and parents, we all strive to honor our children when we truly behold them without judgment. As mentors, acceptance and unconditional love deepen our perceptions, compassion, and understanding.

A hard lesson for me is resisting the temptation to jump in with suggestions and solutions. I have learned to ask, "Would you like to hear what other teachers have tried in this situation?" Collective wisdom can sometimes make new awareness more accessible.

There are many resources at hand for teachers about curriculum and child development. Colleagues, administration, or professionals offer crucial social-emotional, physical, and spiritual support. I learned from participating in nonviolent communication courses to ask this important question: "What do you need to do your job well?" I have repeatedly experienced how this question leads to thoughtful reflection. This question very effectively served to resolve an ongoing conflict at a school where the new administration and teachers were at odds. We gathered in a large circle with faculty and administration. As the school mentor, I facilitated and took notes while each person in turn spoke to that question and added who or what could meet that need—all without discussion. Because everyone had spoken with heartfelt honesty, and the notes were available to everyone concerned, the process was ultimately healing.

I become sincerely interested in the well-being of the mentee and often remind them of Steiner's words about teaching the child to sleep and breathe (Steiner 2013b, lecture I). Inquiring about their own understanding of sleeping and breathing can awaken a conversation about the importance of self-care to be a healthy role model for the children.

I often also ask, "How do you begin your day? And do you have a spiritual practice?" When I am asking these questions, I often share an old folktale about two travelers who grant a poor, kind-hearted couple the gift of continuing whatever they begin in the morning throughout the entire day (Pyle 1965, "How the Good Gifts Were Used by Two").

The mentor's role calls for honesty, tact, and courage. Ideally, a conversation leads to self-awareness by the mentee before the mentor must be explicit about the challenges. Waldorf teachers are called to develop extraordinary mindfulness about each moment in the classroom. I remember when our school mentor kindly asked me, "Anna, what is your thinking behind that activity?" Her question still inspires me.

Once, I was asked to mentor a teacher who was concerning to the school. As I observed him it became clear why this was so. But what could I say? I had read Lorna Byrne's *Angels in My Hair*, and loved her statement, "There are many unemployed angels." So, I called on the angels and when it came time for the conversation, I found myself asking, "What would you rather be doing?" Miraculously, it was just right, cleared the air, and since he had a ready response, we made immediate arrangements for him to move out of the position into a more suitable one. I am often astonished by the help that comes from the spiritual worlds when I remember to ask, and even when I don't ask!

In the classroom, I attend to the quality of the teacher's voice and its effect on the children. Waldorf education values speech: teacher trainings and lucky schools include this in teacher education. But what if one has not had that instruction, practice, or even awareness about tone, timbre, or vocabulary? What is the best way to suggest the improvement of this remarkable human gift? Once I was so surprised by the sentimental, saccharine telling of a story by a teacher that I couldn't resist asking if that were the teacher's true voice. This opened a conversation of what is often an unconscious and sensitive area of awareness for the teacher.

Sometimes, the mentor is the one who can speak to an obvious dilemma that no one has the courage to address. I ask the administrator if there is something I could say anew that has been said often to the faculty to no avail. I also ask teachers if there is anything I can say to the administration that may have been stated and seemingly not heard. As mentor I have the best interest of the whole at heart.

Essential in the mentoring process is the mentor's willingness to do their own inner work. Any approach suggested for the mentee is equally valuable for the mentor, beginning with the question of availability. "Am I available to be present, to observe and listen?"

"How are you doing now?" one often wonders afterward. The sense of responsibility for the total well-being of the school, the teacher, and the class runs deep. What happens after the conversation and the visit can remain a mystery. Who or what is accountable for what transpired between the mentor and the mentee? Depending on the agreed-upon arrangement, is there a follow-up meeting?

Yet each encounter with a mentee is complete in its own unique way. If we never meet again, the authenticity of our presence, attention, and trust will have opened a space where we each feel heard, seen, and met. It might be just a moment of recognition that carries a lifetime of warmth and hopeful new possibilities.

10. "Weaving Together" in the Nursery and Kindergarten: Mentoring an Assistant Teacher

Allison Carroll

In thinking about my experiences working both with and as an assistant teacher, a verse from a beloved spring song comes to mind:

> Weave together
>
> Straw and feather,
>
> Each one doing their best.

Through our "weaving together," a cozy nest can be built for the children that allows them to grow and thrive. How we do this weaving is of the utmost importance. The children are watching, and take nourishment from our gestures, inner mood, and our deeds.

In its essence, the role of the assistant teacher is to support the children and the lead teacher. How this is done and what this entails will vary. Mentoring a teacher one works with daily presents unique challenges. Offering feedback in the moment is not always possible because the children or other colleagues may be present. One-on-one mentoring meetings can be difficult to maintain. It can be uncomfortable to give feedback to a person one works with every day. An assistant teacher may have more experience in certain areas than the lead teacher.

Five potential trouble spots:

1) Micromanaging by the lead teacher

2) Giving an assistant all of the cleaning duties

3) When or how to give feedback to the assistant

4) Lack of openness to feedback by the assistant

5) Not looking ahead to the future

As a lead teacher, I am guilty of at times micromanaging even though I was never subjected to this as an assistant teacher. Instead, I was given an initial training and then left somewhat to my own devices to observe and take in all that was offered by observing the way the lead teachers worked with the children, families, colleagues, our classroom materials and space, and in nature. I was given great trust to participate and collaborate on many levels, and there was always an eye to my future.

I was encouraged to memorize and tell fairy tales, present puppet shows, attend parent conferences, join committees; assist with interviews, open houses, festivals, public marionette performances; and attend professional conferences. I was not there only to make snack, do the laundry, and clean the classroom, but was instead treated as a valued colleague and lead teacher in training.

I was deeply nourished by this way of working and loved being left free to watch and learn and to support the lead teacher and the children. And I knew from my fellow assistants from teacher training, who worked at other schools, that this was not always the case. Some felt that all they did was cook and clean, or that they did nothing right. Others felt they had no guidance at all, and yet were at times left in charge of the class.

As I reflect upon my own mentoring of an assistant as a lead teacher, I see the need for more one-on-one meetings and a commitment to the future. I want to ask myself, on an ongoing basis, "What does my assistant need to practice next, to round out their experience?" Perhaps it is circle time or singing, gestures or parent work. Then it is on me to ensure I provide an opportunity for that practice to happen, and one-on-one meetings to plan and review these activities. This would provide a very natural way to offer feedback.

Our relationship as lead and assistant teachers is almost like that of two parents. We have to support each other in every moment. We rely upon each other. And we nurture and care for each other. This is a gift for the children, even if we do not always get it right.

Like the song, we have a chance to "weave together straw and feather," and bring our best selves to our work with the children and each other. Mentoring is an important part of this relationship, and it is worth considering and evaluating how we are taking that up. The future of Waldorf education, as well as the children in our care and our dear colleagues, will all benefit if we do.

11. Mentoring and Evaluating: Similarities and Differences

Louise deForest

In the Pedagogical Section at the Goetheanum newsletter a few years ago, Aina Aasland, Florian Osswald, and colleagues shared the International Teacher Education Project, which is a set of guidelines for teacher education, based on feedback from colleagues all over the world (Aasland 2020). In it, eight fields have been identified as key components for teacher development for those working with the youngest to the oldest children in our schools. These eight guidelines represent the ideal we all strive toward as teachers, and all of these fields chart the transformative process of the journey of the teacher. The learning process will not be uniform, but can be used to help identify strengths and areas needing support. They are as follows:

1) Development of knowledge practices: consciously following a sequential path of self-development allowing one to experience and identify one's own thinking.

2) The arts: this allows us to develop insight into ourselves, the other, and the world. It links thinking, feeling, and willing, and acts as a bridge between inner and outer experience. Through the arts, self-transformation becomes possible.

3) Self-development: conferences, classes, study, meditative practice, etc.

4) Research: investigating and expanding the changing picture and understanding of children and education. Special needs children, racial identities, cultural and religious beliefs, and issues of gender identity are all areas of life today that need further exploring. If we can identify and relate phenomena, we will deepen and broaden our understanding, knowledge, and practice.

5) Basic knowledge: literacy, numeracy, and oral skills. A general understanding of social and cultural contexts.

6) Teaching and learning: the understanding of a developmentally appropriate and responsive curriculum and practical work.

7) Expanding understanding of human nature: an understanding of the human being that embraces the tangible and intangible. A phenomenological approach that seeks to understand the full spectrum of human experience.

8) Education and societal change: examining other forms of education and investigating what might become appropriate in the future. Entertaining the question of how we can change our practice to better meet children coming toward us from the future. Entering a dialogue with other educational systems and approaches, and exploring the potential of education to facilitate social change. Working with parents, social and cultural equity, discrimination, social justice, accessibility, inherent biases, etc.

All of the above are relevant to every teacher in every section of the school or program. We are all on the same path!

For both mentors and evaluators, these eight fields should be living in our inner and outer work. We cannot ask a new teacher to be doing what we ourselves are not doing. And of course, this is all in the context of anthroposophy, not a dogmatic anthroposophy, but a thoughtful anthroposophy that can enable a new teacher to grow in accordance with essential qualities of this education and find a context for their questions, observations, and generational impulses.

Mentor

A mentor is someone who is committed to accompanying a teacher over time, entering into a relationship of trust and, ideally, mutual respect. Mentoring is a relationship where both parties can learn and grow; indeed, a productive mentoring relationship is really only positive when both teachers learn from each other and where both can engage in flexible and creative thinking. A mentor strives to support the teacher in finding their own way of teaching and often can see something, a potential capacity or gift in the mentee's work, of which they are not yet aware. It is important that the mentor recognizes and respects the fact that the new teacher is also bringing new impulses and their own karmic tasks to this work.

When I think of how I best learn, it is not through someone pointing out my mistakes (though that can be helpful if it is nonjudgmental) or telling me how it "should" be done, but rather through the confidence that person has in my abilities and through the questions they ask of me ("Why did you choose that story for this group?" or "How do you think that circle went?"). In asking these types of questions, the mentor can help bring the theory into practice and can guide the mentee into the inner realm of the "why" behind what we do.

In many ways, it's like what we as teachers strive to do in the classroom. If we show infinite confidence in a child, especially if this child is challenged behaviorally; if we search to see beyond the behavior to the being of the child and the roots of said behavior, before long that child will strive to live up to our good opinion, and the confidence I feel in that child will become their own self-confidence. When an experienced teacher sees the inevitable mistakes we make as newer teachers (and experienced teachers will be quick to tell you that they make mistakes every day), the days when everything falls apart, and still has confidence in us, that makes a difference. It gives us strength to keep striving.

> *How did the rose ever open its heart and give to the world all its beauty? It felt the encouragement of light against its being; otherwise, we all remain too frightened.*
>
> —Hafiz

"There is no education other than self-education," said Rudolf Steiner. Just as in any other teaching situation, we must overcome certain aspects of ourselves to be effective teachers. Essentially, mentoring is not about showing how much we know but about helping another unfold what they know.

To be an effective mentor and evaluator, one needs to overcome the conditions of our times. We know that in the effort to give birth to the Consciousness Soul, we draw into ourselves more and more, becoming more individualized in the process, becoming more and more closed within our own reality. Every aspect of working within an anthroposophical community pushes us to bring to consciousness what our tasks are now, for these times. For a mentoring relationship to be effective and positive, it is vital for the mentor to overcome certain characteristics of our times.

Develop interest in the other: "Who are you?" should be our question as mentors, "And what brings you to this work?" What are the impulses from the future that this teacher brings and how can I foster them? How can I serve you?

Overcoming sympathy and antipathy: liking or not liking a mentee is never an option, just as with the children in our care. We are not there as mentors to judge the other; we are there to serve and to grow with the other.

It is a very modern attribute, to look for what is wrong. Our intellect is always looking for the flaw, always dividing and reducing. Can we find where the other shines? What does this new teacher do better than you have ever done? Even if they are awkward, can you see the striving? Is there something that you can wholeheartedly applaud?

As modern human beings, we tend to want to fix situations, to look for the solution to problems. Carrying and uncovering questions, rather than giving answers, can help us move beyond this into something more profound and infinitely more useful. Everything is an open question. Often the biggest "problems" have a doorway into insights we know nothing about.

In the materialistic world of today, how things look is often given more emphasis than how things are, and wanting to look good takes precedence over being good. How many times have we all been asked to clean up the school for a parent evening, rather than for the children for whom the school is a second home? Waldorf education is all about an inner gesture, rather than a fixed way of doing.

In overcoming the inner challenges of our times, we can meet each other in a truer and more heart-filled space and develop social understanding, which Rudolf Steiner tells us is essential for the development of the Consciousness Soul.

Recognize that we are all in a process of becoming, and that the mentoring we do with an inexperienced teacher is a process and will not necessarily yield immediate results. Give them space to make mistakes and to discover their own path and way of teaching over time.

Now is the time to know that all you do is sacred. Now is the time to understand that all your ideas of right and wrong were just a child's training wheels, to be laid aside, when you can finally live with veracity and love.

—*Hafiz*

Evaluator

When trying to differentiate between the tasks of the mentor and the tasks of an evaluator, it can be helpful to ask yourself, as a mentor, who am I accountable to? And as an evaluator, to whom am I answerable? You'll often find very different answers to those two questions.

While a mentor is all about a process in time and a relationship, an evaluator acts more as an objective mirror to show the teacher where they are right now. There is a short process but ideally no personal relationship between the evaluator and the teacher, and once the evaluation visit is over that is usually the end of any formal contact between the two.

Just like the mentor, an evaluator can feel compassion and warmth toward the new teacher, especially remembering the long journey it has been to achieve some proficiency in their own work, but the evaluator works from a provisional commitment to the school, and even more, to assure the quality of Waldorf education in the world.

I have always preferred to remain apart from the daily activity of the classroom when I am both mentoring and evaluating a teacher. This allows me to quietly observe instead of interacting, though often children will come up to me and ask who I am (and whose grandmother I am). This way, it is far easier for me to get a feeling for the whole room and each activity, to sense the mood of the room, and to perceive the relationship between the teacher and their class and, when outside, with the teacher's colleagues. I can observe how the parents drop off or pick up their children; are they greeted by the teacher? Is there warmth in the greeting, or fear? Are the parents comfortable in the school and in front of the teacher? As with mentoring, one tries to eliminate all judgments attached to these observations and to just see the reality.

As an evaluator, it is important for you to define for yourself what it is you feel is essential. What are you looking for? And what was missing in the day that you expected to see? Many of our observations will be based on an intuitive perception, not so much what a person does as the inner gesture and mood and warmth body in the classroom. Does the day breathe? Can the teacher feel when the children need to have a change of activity, or do they plow through with their plan for the morning? Often, a teacher can have lots of knowledge but no feel for or connection to the group.

And how much of what I see is due to nervousness? For many teachers, there is a lot of stress around an evaluation visit, and often a teacher can feel that their job is at risk. Many teachers are not used to having visitors in their classroom, and they can feel too exposed or vulnerable. Often, too, teachers or a school will put on a show for the visiting evaluator, wining and dining the visitor until they have lost all sense of reality. In all these situations, we must learn to look beyond the nervousness or fear (or comfort) and remain objective.

I have found that occasionally, a school has an ulterior motive for asking someone to evaluate a teacher. Unbeknownst to you, a decision about that teacher has already been made and the school is looking to you to confirm that decision. I can usually discern that this is the case when the school gives me too much information about the person I have come to evaluate. The school expresses concern about the teacher and then goes on to list all the reasons they are concerned. When this happens, I find that I go into the classroom looking for behavior that supports those concerns, thereby losing my objectivity. Perhaps the school has been very straightforward with the teacher, but the teacher has not been able to hear what is being said, or perhaps there is a personal vendetta or scapegoating happening, but it always puts the evaluator in a difficult position. When this has happened, I have been very clear with the school that I will not be used to alleviate a difficult situation in the school; I will write what I see. For this reason, the less information I have, the more comfortable I am, and can walk into the classroom with an open mind, expecting to experience a flowing, breathing early childhood morning.

After both mentoring and evaluation visits, a report is written, shared, and discussed with the teacher. After a mentoring visit, perhaps you want to have the teacher work with certain questions or read specific articles or lectures, and you can include that in the report. I have also included recommendations in an evaluation report, especially if I want the school to support the teacher in following through with them. But there is a big difference between the two reports. The mentoring report is to support the mentee in their ongoing journey into teaching, and it is given to the teacher, not the school. If the mentee is a student at a teacher training institution and you have been assigned by that institution to be the mentor of that student, the report also goes to the director of the program your mentee attends. An evaluation report, however, is a document that is sent to the school, is saved in the teacher's file, and is the property of the school, so it is a much more public document. In writing your report, you should bear this in mind.

One of the complaints that I have heard from schools over the years is that the evaluation reports are often missing specifics, and we are too diplomatic with each other for the document to be really helpful. This is understandable because we are all colleagues, some with more experience than others, but all rooted in the same work and on the same path. However, the evaluation report should be to the point, clear, and matter of fact, simply pointing out where the teacher's strengths lie and where they still need to grow and deepen. This report is shared and discussed with the teacher before being submitted to the school, and many times the teacher can be defensive about your observations or truly not understand what you observed. On occasion, I have changed my report, having misunderstood something I observed, but usually I do not, though I note in the report when the teacher has not agreed with me. Everything in the report—the commendations and the recommendations—has been discussed with the teacher and the professional development committee before it is submitted in writing to the school, so there are no unpleasant surprises. I do not usually make any recommendations about the teacher continuing in the school or not, but there have been times and circumstances where I have suggested finding a more administrative position for a teacher in the future.

I would like to point out one circumstance where mentoring and evaluating should remain very separate. A teacher should never evaluate anyone with whom they have had a mentoring relationship. However tempting it might be, there is just too much of a conflict of interest for the mentor, and the delicate and intimate relationship between the mentor and the mentee runs the risk of being badly damaged. If the mentor-mentee relationship has been as described, the mentor cannot possibly be objective and may, unwittingly, be swayed by the confidences shared over the years with the mentee. This mentor is far too close and knows far too much to ever be able to give an objective evaluation of this mentee.

In closing, I would like to suggest that to listen and to witness, with a caring heart, another's process of discovery and growth may be one of the greatest services that a human being can offer to another. And to give our complete attention to another with warm interest may be the greatest gift we can give and receive.

We are all just walking each other home.

—*Ram Das*

Part II.
Professional Review and Evaluation in Waldorf Early Childhood Education

12. Why Review?

Review and evaluation can ideally help us see ourselves more fully—not only our weaknesses, but also what we do well and take for granted. We have the opportunity to be recognized for our gifts as well as our struggles. A healthy process, however, will also present the opportunity for us to face the reality of habits, attitudes, or points of view in which we may be stuck, perhaps unconsciously. What is revealed can be the boost or shove that we need to continue developing. Waldorf teaching is a profession where one never arrives, but the truth can propel us forward toward a fuller destiny.

The review of the day is an individual meditative practice for Waldorf educators. As groups of educators, perhaps in faculty meetings, we also participate in review when we look back together at our year, at a festival or a specific area of our work. Colleagues should also visit one another's classrooms and, in subsequent conversations, offer observations and suggestions. This kind of peer review, whether it is formal or informal, can build appreciation and trust among colleagues and strengthen all of our classroom practices. In this situation, one could say that we take turns being "moons" for one another.

A professional review or evaluation process requires, in addition to the above kinds of review, the perspective of someone from outside the school. In the same way that an individual may have a "blind spot," an early childhood group may also not be able to see itself clearly. It is also true that if difficult things have to be said, it is easier for someone outside of the group to speak them.

On the other hand, information from colleagues and others will help to fill in the picture of what has transpired over the course of the past weeks, months, and years. The goal of the professional review is a greater objectivity that arises out of the integration of various reflections on the teacher being evaluated. In some cases, it may even include those of colleagues and parents.

Without the diverse experiences and views of those people standing around the teacher, the emerging picture would not be as accurate or as complete. Each viewer offers a different mirror, and together the reflections can begin to approach the reality of an individual's professional journey in a helpful way. When there is resistance to a professional review or evaluation, it is often because not all of the perspectives are represented, or because the process is not embedded in the life of the school but seems separate and foreign.

In a healthy evaluation process, the different perspectives balance one another. In the process as a whole, we must also try to balance the qualities of sun and moon, heart and head, the enhancement of professionalism with deepened capacities for keen observation, honest speaking, and active listening.

13. Reflections on Review

Patricia Rubano

Evaluation and review are words that may give rise to ambivalent feelings, if not downright mistrust, in many of us. Perhaps we have experienced review processes that seemed to be a waste of time, or evaluations that were imposed on us as intimidating in nature. As Waldorf teachers, we know that reviewing the day is an important practice, that review of a lesson after sleep is an integral part of the three-day rhythm, and that objectively reviewing specific times in our lives helps to awaken our higher selves. Perhaps all this reviewing can help us prepare for the life review that Rudolf Steiner tells us we will experience in the soul realm after we die. Maybe we should set aside our doubts and take another look at review.

Those of us who regularly reflect on our work find it to be a valuable practice. It helps us, for example, to orient ourselves in our lives, to clarify our intentions and to set goals. The feedback received by the Waldorf Early Childhood Association of North America (WECAN) about the self-study required for membership has demonstrated the value of practicing reflection in a collegial group as well. Colleagues from many schools have expressed appreciation for the opportunity to work together to review and evaluate their programs. How can these positive experiences help us create a culture that values and incorporates review as a normal part of our professional life and serves the development of both the individual and the organization?

A review process that supports professional development will have certain characteristics and may involve more than a one-day visit from an outside evaluator. It will be inclusive, incorporating feedback from the individual being evaluated, and perhaps colleagues and parents, as well as observations from the outside evaluator. It will engender genuine human encounter through conversations about the feedback gathered, in which both the gifts and the struggles of the individual are acknowledged. The individual educator and the institution will both be accountable for following up on the evaluation, the teacher by taking up the suggestions and the school by supporting the teacher. Finally, when there are serious questions about how well suited a teacher may be for the task at hand, there will be honest dialogue about what may need to change.

Change is never easy, and facing the need to change can invoke fear in all of us. "What will happen if I need to change how I am working with the children, with the parents, or with my colleagues? What will happen if I need to change from my present position to another, or if I need to change my profession altogether?" It is often the case that we already know that change is needed, but don't know how to proceed. If so, wouldn't we want to be told and supported by our friends and colleagues?

I believe that the changes we all really want to make would be more likely to happen if we regularly checked in with ourselves, received feedback from colleagues, and were expected to be accountable for making those changes. Even if we require support from our colleagues, the impulse for change would be experienced as coming from within ourselves rather than being forced on us from the outside. When we are open about our struggles, we might be surprised at how quickly a colleague is willing to compensate for our weakness in a certain area. Out of our strengths in other areas, we can offer the same support to someone else. A body of teachers working together in this way is more than just the sum of its individual parts. This harmonious working of an early childhood department can be an example to the entire school and a gift to the Waldorf early childhood movement as a whole.

This description of review may seem an impractical and idealistic picture. After all, who of us is free from sympathies and antipathies? Who of us has overcome our own critical and judgmental nature? One reason we are afraid of the judgments of others may be because those judgments live in us as well. Compensating for one another is what we do naturally, and we can do it without resentment if we do it consciously and openly. With regard to the fear of feedback from others, I have very rarely given or received a reflection that was not already familiar. In fact, it is the positive reflection that is more often surprising and even difficult to accept. We deprive ourselves of receiving the appreciation of others when we do not find ways to incorporate regular forms of review into our organizations. Over time, it is possible to build enough trust to allow others to give us a fuller picture of ourselves than we could ever achieve on our own.

14. Cultivating Review

How a community prepares for and takes up self-development and shares responsibility for everyone's continued professional growth depends on several factors. A critical one is the prevailing attitude toward review and evaluation. If evaluation is viewed as a process in which everyone's job is on the line, it will likely produce anxiety and defensiveness. If it is seen as a means of professional renewal and a support for teacher development, then it will evoke different and decidedly more helpful responses.

The existing mood or attitude may have arisen out of previous experiences; if they were negative, the group may need to work slowly to rebuild the "soil" again. The group could begin by practicing review in a regular way and by sharing with one another their individual successes at daily review. Another way to become more comfortable with review is for each faculty member to articulate and share their own professional goals with colleagues in the fall. Committing to a yearly self-evaluation in relation to one's stated goals in the spring would be a logical next step in the goal-setting process and bring it to a natural completion.

In general, it is always easier and less complicated to use evaluators from outside the community, for the reasons discussed in the previous chapter. There are some large faculties that have successfully completed evaluations on one another. A teacher, however, must never be asked to evaluate a teacher that they are mentoring. The mentoring relationship is one of support and confidentiality.

Using an outside evaluator provides a certain natural objectivity to the professional review. The view of the outside person, however, is limited by the short span of the visit. This fact may be compensated for by finding a way for the teacher to receive feedback from others as well and by including the self-evaluation of the teacher in the final report of the evaluator. In this way the professional review process will represent not just one person's view or a momentary snapshot of the situation, but a more complete picture of a teacher's journey and life within the school community.

Clarity in the steps of the process, clarity about the timeline, and clarity about who does what are also essential to building a healthy culture of review. There must be no hidden agendas on the part of the group that manages the professional development and evaluation work. The group in charge also needs to be mindful of avoiding sympathy and antipathy and allow the process to bring to light the necessary information. Practicing listening to one another without judging or jumping to conclusions is a helpful exercise for anyone who works in a collegial group.

Using an evaluation in a crisis situation, where colleagues already have serious questions about a teacher's capability, presents a special challenge. However, in such a case, it is better to have a process that includes an outside evaluation than to have no process at all. What we are trying to cultivate, ideally, is a regular rhythm of review and evaluation for all colleagues in a school or center. An informal partnering of peers or buddies can also help build skills in observing and in sharing among colleagues.

Time and timing have to be considered in many different ways. All teachers should know well in advance what is expected of them and when it is expected. Processes that are rushed often create more problems than solutions. Predictable rhythms are healthy and help review and evaluation find their natural place in the life of the organization.

Time needs to be allowed for the educator to complete a thoughtful self-evaluation. Asking questions in the process of looking at one's own work creates a greater possibility of openness to the observations and suggestions of a visitor. It is ideal if the teacher being evaluated and the evaluator have a chance for a conversation before the classroom visit. The evaluator, having already read the teacher's self-evaluation, can ask further questions. The teacher has the opportunity to ask the evaluator to focus on one or another area of the teacher's own questions during the visit. This conversation, even if it is brief, builds a sense of collaborative inquiry.

The post-visit conversation between the evaluator and the teacher is most important. At this time the teacher should receive the significant observations and recommendations from the evaluator that later will be delivered in a written report or orally to the evaluating body. A teacher should not read significant recommendations in a written report that have not already been shared in a post-visit conversation. In some processes, the teacher is given time to review the written evaluation report and respond in writing as well. But it is in the face-to-face meetings between the teacher and the evaluator that the most benefit can be realized. This is also true of a teacher's meeting with colleagues at the end of an evaluation, when the recommendations are discussed. The feeling of earnest support for one's striving by one's fellow teachers is like rain and sun for tender seedlings!

Willingness to reveal ourselves and to trust our circle of colleagues comes as a result of taking care of all the stages of a professional development process in an educational setting, but especially in those activities connected to evaluation. Cultivating a ground in which questions of self-development are embraced, rather than avoided, is an important precondition that influences every other aspect of the professional review process. It must not be overlooked.

15. The Self-Evaluation

How can a professional review process, in itself, be an opportunity for learning, not only for the educator in question, but also for everyone involved?

The educator's self-reflection should be at the heart of the process. While the common mechanical analogy for the heart is that of a pump, Rudolf Steiner helped us to understand that the heart is really much more an organ of perception. Its activity is the result of what it senses to be happening in the rest of the body. Like the heart, the self-evaluation component of the review process needs to be sensitive, responsive, and adaptable to changing circumstances, and, on a soul level, inspiring.

Thus, we've devised a set of forms that are intended to also embody these qualities. The self-evaluation questionnaires (long and short form) in the appendix to this book are models that can be used as presented, modified to suit different circumstances, or expanded and contracted from one year to the next, depending on the needs of individuals or institutions.

At some time in our lives, most of us have been asked the question, "What are your strengths and weaknesses?" While such a question might lead one to a revelation, there is a kind of yes/no, either/ or duality inherent in the question itself. All Waldorf educators are on a continuing, lifelong path of development. Moreover, we know that sometimes our strengths are also our weaknesses; a strength in one situation may prove to be unhelpful in another and vice versa. Knowing that we will never really arrive at the high ideals toward which we are striving also makes it difficult, at times, to trust our perspective on where we have been or where we ought to be going.

All of this underscores the reality that it matters what questions are asked. The areas highlighted in both the long and the short self-evaluation questionnaires are derived from "The Essentials of Waldorf Early Childhood Education" by Susan Howard (chapter 3).

In the long form, under each area are four questions. Two of these are connected to the educator's own intentions and consciousness. The other two in each section ask the educator to look at the children, parents, or colleagues for information about his or her work. Answering the questions requires that one alternate between an inward and an outward focus. This flow of communication between the center and the periphery is another way in which the self-evaluation is connected to the image of the human heart.

There are two other ways in which the image of the heart is relevant. The heart "knows," in a different way than the head, what is true and what is real. Information brought to light out of dialogue and relationship can complement what one observes, or the facts of the situation. In the heart, this sense for the truth is complemented by the capacity for love. The questionnaires may be imperfect and far from reaching their intended goal, but if those who take them up give to the process something out of their own hearts, then both individuals and the community will grow.

USING THE SELF-EVALUATION QUESTIONNAIRES

The Long Form

The long form of the self-evaluation questionnaire can be used as an individual or early childhood department self-study, or it can become the central component of the early childhood educator professional review process.

When it is a required part of the professional review, the timeline for completion of the long form should be sufficient, and what is expected of the educator should be made clear. Responding to the questions in a significant way necessitates ample time to make observations and to document one's observations, reflections, and insights. The completed questionnaire should be given to the evaluator prior to the classroom visit. Time should also be allowed for conversation between the teacher who completed the questionnaire and the evaluator, ideally both before and after the classroom visit.

The Short Form

The short form of the self-evaluation questionnaire can be used in the same ways as the long form. While it covers all of the same areas of focus as the long form, each section asks one question instead of four questions. While it is less time intensive to complete, it can also be expanded to meet the particular needs of a situation by adding questions from each section of the long form or by adding all of the questions in one or more sections to what is contained in the short form. This might be done when an early childhood group wants to penetrate an area of its work more deeply, or if the professional development committee feels that an individual's work in a certain area has demonstrated a need for more attention.

Creating Your Own Questionnaire

The sample questions that follow are designed as examples of how a self-evaluation form can also be a learning process. It is our hope that early childhood educators will find that taking up these questions is an inspiration for their work. The questionnaire can be tailored to meet the specific needs of any early childhood group. Even the process of modifying the form can be a valuable and educative exercise for a group of colleagues. It might also be valuable to research what other schools use for self-evaluation forms, thus broadening the picture.

SAMPLE QUESTIONS: EARLY CHILDHOOD EDUCATOR SELF-EVALUATION

The full forms, both long and short, are in the appendix.

Ongoing Self-Development

- Describe your present areas of study and your inner work in relation to your task as an educator. Include a description of how you prepare for your class.

- What questions are you carrying?

- List your professional goals for the year.

- What professional development activities (workshops, conferences, mentoring, visits to other educators) have you undertaken during the last three years?

Cultivating a Mood for the Young Child

- What aspects of your work give you the greatest joy?

- Of what are you most appreciative?

- How is joy manifested in the children and in your day with the children?

- In what ways do gratitude, reverence, and wonder live in the physical and social environment?

Being Worthy of Imitation

- In what ways do you see yourself reflected positively in the mirror of the children's behavior?

- In what area do you have to work consciously every day to be a worthy model for the children?

- How is meaningful adult activity practiced in your classroom? In what ways?

- In what ways are healthy social relations modeled?

Life-Filled Activity as the Heart of Early Childhood Education

- What is the most creative aspect of the work for you? How do you find renewal for your own creative forces?

- How do you balance practical work, artistic, and play activities for the children? How do you try to balance the needs of the group and the needs of the individuals in your class?

- How can you tell from the children themselves that there is a healthy flow and balance in the structure and rhythms of the day and week?

- Give an example of how the children demonstrate that they are secure enough in their surroundings to bring forth individual creative impulses, especially in play.

Nourishing Growth and Development

- If you are working with a mixed-age group, how do you adjust what you bring and your expectations to the different ages of the children? How do you do the same with diversity among your students?

- How are you working consciously to support in the children development of the senses of touch, life, movement, and balance?

- In what ways do you experience that the children in your class are thriving?

- Are there individual children about whom you have concerns or questions? How are you addressing these concerns or questions? Do you have the support and/or resources that you need to address them?

Creating a Circle of Warmth and Love

- In what ways are you consciously trying to create warmth, love, and inclusion in the physical environment, in the children's daily activities, in social relations, and in the handling of disruptive or challenging behavior?

- How does this circle include the parents of the children in your care?

- How would you characterize your relations with your colleagues?

- What contribution do you make to the school community as a whole?

The Art of Listening and the Practice of Collaboration

- Describe how you and your colleagues work with child study. How are you honing your skills in child observation?

- How do you deal with conflict in collegial relations or in situations where you disagree with existing decisions or policies?

- What is most rewarding in your work with parents? What is most challenging?

- How are you cultivating a spiritual connection to the children in your care?

Final Questions

- Is there a picture or an image that captures your year, your class, or this process for you?

- What do you hope to gain from this review process?

- Is there anything else that you want to share with others who will be receiving this information?

16. The Role of the Evaluator

A visitor to an early childhood classroom can bring a great deal of delight to the children, especially if the visitor slips in unobtrusively and is as happy to be there as the children are to have a guest. Imagine, on the other hand, how it might be for the children and their teacher to host a frowning, tight-lipped "know-it-all!" While many stories may include such a hard-hearted character and the challenge that it represents, we would not choose such an archetype to be our evaluator.

Experience in Waldorf early childhood settings is not the only necessary qualification for an evaluator. There are specific qualities, capacities, and skills that an individual serving as an evaluator will want to cultivate.

Honesty is paramount. Openness, genuineness, sincerity, frankness, fairness, trustworthiness, and acting in an honorable manner are all embedded in the meaning of the word. Much of what an evaluator would aspire to could be found in this expanded definition of honesty, especially when it is coupled with the capacity for tactful communication.

Rudolf Steiner advised the teachers of the first Waldorf School to "have courage for the truth." He linked having courage for the truth to two other activities that are also relevant to our topic.

> *Imbue thyself with the power of imagination,*
> *Have courage for the truth,*
> *Sharpen thy feeling for responsibility of soul.*
>
> —*Rudolf Steiner,* The Study of Man

An evaluator's capacity to sense the truth finds its basis in an understanding of essential principles, while avoiding fixed notions of how those principles must be manifested in a particular situation. It is through the creative power of the imagination that the evaluator can recognize and celebrate an individual educator's artistic expression of common understandings. An evaluator will also be keenly aware of the deep responsibility of serving as a guide for the development of a fellow educator.

We offer below a checklist that outlines the different stages of the evaluation visit and questions to be considered at each stage.

CHECKLIST FOR THE EVALUATOR

This form is replicated in full in the appendix.

Preparation for the Visit

- Am I inwardly and outwardly prepared for the evaluation visit?
- Do I have copies of all the relevant material?
- Do I know what the school expects of me?
- Do I know to what group or committee I am responsible?
- Do I know how to reach my contact person (phone and email) at the school?
- Have I read the teacher's self-evaluation?
- Have I set up a phone conversation or a meeting with the teacher prior to my visit?
- Do I have a schedule for my visit?
- Am I conscious of the teacher's questions as well as the questions of the school?

Initial Meeting with the Teacher

- How did I help us form a positive working relationship prior to the observation?
- Did we review the teacher's self-evaluation together?
- Did I ask the teacher about additional questions?
- Did I ask the teacher if there was anything that they would like me to observe?
- Was I able to listen without jumping to conclusions?
- Is my interest in this person genuine?

The Classroom Observation

- Did I arrange with the teacher where to sit and what to do to be less obtrusive?
- Did I take in impressions without falling into sympathy or antipathy?
- Did I make observations objectively?
- Was I able to be inwardly calm?
- Was I able to bring myself into the right mood for the children?
- Was I a supportive presence for the teacher?

The Post-Observation Conversation

- Were there sufficient time and a private space for an in-depth conversation?

- Did I ask the teacher if the day was typical or not?

- Did I allow the teacher to speak first?

- Did I offer my observations before offering any interpretations?

- Did I ask the teacher to explain why certain things were done as they were?

- Did I share out of my own experiences?

- Did I refrain from overwhelming the teacher with multiple suggestions?

- Was I honest in sharing my concerns?

- Did we agree on concrete objectives?

- Were we able to find, together, a key to the teacher's future development?

The Written Report

- Were my communications clear, professional, and addressed to the appropriate persons?

- Did I ask the teacher to review the report for inaccuracies?

- Was there a fair balance of commendations and recommendations in the report?

- Were specific goals, timelines, and support suggested in the report?

- Were options for professional development opportunities noted when appropriate?

- Did I respect agreements for confidentiality?

Even for experienced evaluators, who may already have internalized such a list, the questions above can still serve as useful reminders. For educators who are new to the task of evaluation, the checklist can help them become successful guides for others.

SAMPLE QUESTIONS FOR A RECORD OF OBSERVATIONS BY THE EVALUATOR

These questions are reproduced in the "Record of Observations by the Evaluator" form in the appendix. They correlate to the questions on the self-evaluation questionnaire. A copy of the completed self-evaluation questionnaire should be attached to this record of observations and to the evaluation report. These, too, are all available as forms in the appendix.

Mood for the Young Child

How is the early childhood educator cultivating a mood of joy, gratitude, wonder, and reverence for the young child? How do these qualities manifest in the educator, in the environment, and in the social life in the class?

Being Worthy of Imitation

How is the early childhood educator working at being worthy of imitation, both in the areas of natural strengths and gifts and in areas that are more challenging?

Life-Filled Activity

How does the rhythm of the day provide for a balance of practical work, artistic activity, and creative play? How does the early childhood educator balance the needs of the class and those of individual children?

Nourishing Growth and Development

How do the children demonstrate that they are thriving? How is the early childhood educator working to help the children develop their senses of touch, life, movement, and balance? Is the diversity that lives among the children acknowledged and worked with in the environment and in everyday activities? Are there developmental needs of individual children or a group of children that appear to need attention?

Creating a Circle of Warmth and Love

How does the early childhood educator handle social difficulties among the children, or challenging behaviors of individual children? Is there a mood of warmth, inclusivity, and belonging that acknowledges and nourishes the classroom environment, the children, parents, and colleagues? What did you observe about the quality of the relations of the educator with their colleagues and with the parents of the children in the class?

The Art of Listening and the Practice of Collaboration

How does the early childhood educator demonstrate openness to feedback and advice from colleagues or mentors? Is there a specific area of the work that appears to need further development and support?

17. The Role of the Institution

Governance structures in Waldorf schools or early childhood centers are typically based on a collaborative model. Regarding evaluation, this usually means that a faculty or staff as a whole or a core group (such as the College of Teachers) has a primary responsibility for the quality of the educational programs. Each school will determine how this responsibility can best be fulfilled. Certain functions may be mandated to individuals or to a committee—for example, a professional development committee—but ideally, all of the staff will feel a sense of responsibility for one another's continued professional development.

Individual members of a faculty will participate in carrying this responsibility in accordance with their particular capacities and skills. Some staff members, for example, may facilitate the professional review process; others may participate by giving requested feedback to colleagues; still others may support colleagues in areas that have been identified as needing to be strengthened. Knowing who is responsible for the professional review processes in any organization is essential, and the responsible group will also need to have a clear mandate that describes its role and its relations to other groups, as well as its decision-making authority.

Chapter 14, "Cultivating Review," described the importance of cultivating a healthy environment for both review and evaluation. In a community where teachers practice self-reflection and share their striving with one another, it becomes apparent that everyone is a "work in progress." Giving appropriate and helpful feedback to colleagues also requires practice. When sharing and feedback are understood as a part of an educator's job description, individuals will feel much safer in communicating their struggles and in asking for help.

In a climate that encourages self-reflection and sharing, colleagues know what is happening in classrooms besides their own and have a sense of how things are going in the school as a whole. Mistakes and challenges are then seen as opportunities for learning and improvement, not as reasons for blame or shame. Collegial relationships will tend to be stronger and more resilient; they will be able to weather even the most difficult or delicate communications, when these are delivered in the spirit of collaboration and support. Cultivating this mood is another critical area of attention for the institution.

A further important step is the establishment of regular rhythms and cycles of review and evaluation that can be maintained over time and become a part of the ongoing life of the organization. Regular, rhythmic processes are the best way to notice, before it is too late, what is missing or what needs mending.

Cycles of formal review may vary, occurring anywhere from once a year to once every fourth year. In some schools, self-evaluations and peer visits take place every year, while in alternate years a visit from an outside evaluator is included as a part of the professional review. When an evaluation process includes input from colleagues and parents, sometimes called a "360-degree evaluation," this more extensive process is undertaken only every third or fourth year. In this case, one third or one quarter of the teachers in a school will be participating in a professional review process in any given year. New teachers may expect to participate in a professional review process during their first year and after that on a regular basis.

In addition to designating clear responsibility for the professional review process, creating a healthy culture for review, and establishing regular cycles for evaluation, the role of the institution in the professional review process includes further areas of responsibility, which are included in the following list.

Responsibilities of the Institution for the Professional Review Process:

- Delineate clear responsibility for the professional review process

- Cultivate a positive climate of review and evaluation and foster the capacities and skills needed by participating colleagues

- Establish regular rhythms of review and evaluation to assure adequate support for ongoing teacher development

- Articulate clear expectations, timelines, and protocol in writing and have systems in place to make sure that these are upheld

- Provide support for individual professional development recommended in the written report, including funds for courses, if required

- Assure that adequate mentoring and in-service training opportunities complement review and evaluation processes

Clearly written policies and procedures will help bring review and evaluation processes into the rhythmic life of the organization and assure that everyone knows what is expected of them. These policies may be published in a faculty handbook, distributed during staff orientation, or handed to a new teacher as a part of the hiring and on-boarding processes. It is also helpful to have a conversation each year in the appropriate collegial group to look over and discuss the policies and procedures. As already indicated, an individual or a committee needs to take on the tasks of making sure that timelines and procedures are followed, that outside evaluators are scheduled, and that relevant communications occur in a timely manner.

Communications protocol for self-evaluations, peer visits, and observations by outside evaluators should be clearly spelled out in written policies. For example, the group who receives the self-evaluations, evaluator reports, and other written materials has a responsibility to maintain professional confidentiality. These materials are not to be discussed outside of their meetings. An educator undergoing evaluation and an outside evaluator are also bound to respect agreements regarding confidentiality.

The professional review process is usually overseen by a College of Teachers or by a sub-group of the faculty, such as a personnel or professional development committee. In some schools, the responsibility may even be mandated to an individual or to an executive group with members representing the faculty, board, and administration. Whatever model is chosen, it is important that the group has the trust of their colleagues, that their authority and responsibilities are well defined, and that the group members have been chosen for their capacities to be effective in the work.

Special Considerations for Implementing a 360-Degree Evaluation

If an organization chooses a 360-degree model, in which parents and colleagues are asked for feedback about an individual's work in the school, then special attention must be given to how that part of the process can be handled in a productive and professional manner. Those experienced in this approach suggest that parents and colleagues receive a letter from the group that is overseeing the professional review, clarifying the purpose of the process, the timeline, the form of the feedback, who will be receiving the information, and what will happen to the comments received. This way of inviting feedback should be separate from, and should not be used in the place of, a legal grievance procedure or a conflict resolution process. This distinction should be made clear to all participants. Anonymous feedback is not generally consistent with the intentions of this feedback model. If a parent or a colleague is not willing to sign their name, the concerns must be of such a serious nature that they would warrant being handled by a grievance procedure or a conflict resolution process.

Comments from parents and colleagues are usually sent to the group overseeing the evaluation and, in some cases, to the evaluator. In organizations using this model the comments are summarized for the one undergoing review and shared with them by the evaluator or the responsible group. The summary may become a part of the written report, but typically, the comments received are not included in the teacher's personnel file. Whether the teacher receives copies of the feedback forms or not is a decision that should be made clear prior to the beginning of the process.

In one school where parents are asked to participate in the professional review, the review committee chair writes a letter to the parents, once the review has been completed, thanking them for their help. The educator who has completed the review process approves the letter that is sent to the parents. The letter may describe the process in general terms but does not include specific commendations or recommendations.

Follow-up and Support

Regardless of what model is used, the follow-up and support of the process is nearly as important as the evaluation itself. When all of the relevant information has been received, the responsible group will meet with the teacher being evaluated to review the materials received, including the teacher's self-evaluation and the report of the evaluator. If time permits, the evaluator may be included in this meeting. In any case, the evaluator has already had a post-visit conversation with the teacher and the teacher may already have seen the evaluator's report. In some organizations, the educator being evaluated is also asked, after having read the report, to respond to it in writing. The purpose of the meeting is to review the commendations and recommendations and to determine how best to support the colleague's further growth and development.

The importance of supporting individual educators in areas identified as needing improvement can sometimes be overlooked. Self-knowledge, whether it arises out of self-reflection or the observation of another, is the key to change, but identifying what needs to be transformed is not, in itself, usually sufficient. Most individuals will need continued support during a period of significant professional growth. A concrete, written professional development plan with a timeline can be very effective in helping the responsible group keep track of an individual's progress. It can be equally helpful to the educator to have specific goals and to know that colleagues, through the agreements in the plan, are providing ongoing support toward the realization of those goals.

The last area of responsibility is to note that mentoring and other in-service training opportunities are offered, as a reminder that professional development within an organization includes activities beyond those directly connected to the professional review process. Mentoring is a critical function for the success of new teachers and for the overall health of the programs. Ongoing study of Waldorf educational principles and of the challenges to the child and the family in today's world builds community among colleagues. It deepens our capacities to meet the needs of those who are coming to our schools and early childhood centers.

In describing the role of the evaluator in chapter 16, we offered a checklist of important considerations for the outside evaluator in a professional review process in a Waldorf early childhood setting. Here, we include a checklist that details the many considerations in each of the areas of responsibility for the institution conducting the professional review process. While the list may seem daunting, failure to attend to these details could imperil the whole process.

Checklist for the Institution

This form is included in the appendix.

As an institution, we are cultivating a positive climate of review and evaluation and fostering the capacities and skills needed by participating colleagues.

- The faculty and staff are aware of the importance of review and evaluation as a valuable component of teacher development and as a way of being accountable to one another, to the parents, and to their community.
- As a group, we practice setting goals and reviewing results when appropriate.
- Our faculty agreements encourage direct communication.
- We practice listening to one another in our meetings.
- We are interested in what is going on in our colleagues' classrooms.

We have established regular rhythms of review and evaluation that assure adequate support for ongoing teacher development.

- Teachers expect to participate in regular cycles of self-evaluation, peer visits, and professional review by an outside evaluator.

- Cycles are accommodated in our meeting schedules and other organizational rhythms.

- Parents and board members are aware of the evaluation timelines and procedures.

- Someone is responsible for scheduling and communication concerning evaluations.

- Consideration is given as to whether it would be beneficial to have the outside evaluator visit for more than one day. Time for conversation with the educator being evaluated is built into the schedule of the outside evaluator's visit.

- There is a separate, special policy and procedure for cases of serious concern.

Expectations, timelines, and protocol have been articulated in writing and systems are in place to make sure that the processes are upheld.

- Written policies and procedures for professional review have been distributed to all the early childhood educators and have been discussed in the appropriate collegial groups.

- There is a group who has been mandated to oversee the professional review process.

- Colleagues know where to address questions and concerns about the process.

- There is an established protocol for communication concerning evaluation that has been published and that everyone is expected to follow.

- If parents are asked to participate, they receive clear, written communication about the process and their role. Parents know where to address questions about the process.

- Every outside evaluator has a contact person who makes sure that the evaluator receives all of the relevant materials in a timely way, schedules spaces for meetings, and arranges for the meals and accommodations of the evaluator.

- If there are standard forms for self-evaluations, peer visits, and evaluator reports, these are distributed to those who are expected to complete them by the contact person. Report forms should include space for commendations as well as recommendations.

- There are a procedure and resources in place for the evaluator to be adequately compensated.

The institution provides support for individual professional development recommended in the written report, including funds for courses, if required.

- The educator being evaluated meets with the responsible group to look over the materials that have been collected. Together, they create a professional development plan for the educator that has specific goals and a timeline.

- Support from the institution may include additional mentoring in a specific area, providing an opportunity to visit another teacher's classroom, or offering funds for a summer course or additional training.

- Professional development funds are available for teachers who need additional training.

- Arrangements for additional follow-up meetings are made, if needed.

The institution has adequate mentoring and in-service training opportunities that complement the review and evaluation processes.

- If the teacher being evaluated has a mentor, the mentor should be invited by the responsible group to attend the post-observation conversation or be given a copy of the written report by the teacher.

- Mentors support the teachers they are mentoring by integrating into their mentoring sessions work on the goals articulated in the individual professional development plans.

SAMPLE QUESTIONS FOR COLLEAGUES

For institutions who wish to implement a 360-degree evaluation process, here are some sample questions for colleagues and parents. All questionnaires for colleagues or parents should have a place for the person who fills out the form to sign their name. These questions are reproduced as a form in the appendix.

Appreciations

- In what ways do you value this colleague?

- What gifts does this colleague bring to the school?

Professionalism

- Give examples of this colleague's professionalism or lack of professionalism, e.g., punctuality, reliability, discretion, and respect for confidentiality.

- How well and in what ways does this colleague represent the school to the parents and in the larger community?

Colleagueship

- Has this colleague demonstrated a willingness to work collaboratively? Give examples.

- Does this colleague support other teachers by sharing resources, experience, and skills? Give examples.

Involvement

- How would you describe this colleague's contributions to meetings?

- To what extent does this colleague take on responsibilities in the school beyond caring for their class? In what ways?

Development

- Is this colleague open to feedback or advice? Give examples.

- How does this colleague deal with conflict?

- Have you experienced this colleague's willingness to work on areas that are challenging?

- How?

- Include signature and date.

SAMPLE QUESTIONS FOR PARENTS

- Please describe the quality of communication between you and your child's teacher.

- In what ways have you found the class meetings to be valuable?

- In what ways was the parent/teacher conference helpful to you?

- Do you have any other reflections that you would like to share with your child's teacher?

- Include signature and date.

18. Obstacles and Hindrances

We can expect to encounter challenges along the path of review and evaluation, whether we are educators undergoing a professional review process, evaluators coming into a school or early childhood center, or members of the group in an institution responsible for overseeing the professional development processes of the faculty or staff. Careful consideration of the questions in the checklists offered in the previous chapters can help avoid some of the difficulties that may present themselves.

Now imagine scenarios containing the following fragments of dialogue.

No one told me you were coming.
What Self-Evaluation?
Hi, I'm the substitute.
I have to go home right after class.
It doesn't matter to us what forms you use.
No, we don't know which parent submitted that comment.
We don't have time for a meeting; just send us the report.
What check?

While any of these situations might be no more than a knot in the process, it is more likely that something critical has been overlooked. An effective professional evaluation process is dependent on all of the participants—the teacher, the evaluator, and the responsible group in the institution—being awake to their roles and responsibilities and working cooperatively. If any one of them fails, the other two may have to carry a little extra in order to bring the process to a successful conclusion.

Commonly experienced obstacles and hindrances have been grouped in the following four areas: resistance to change, disparity of expectations, communication difficulties, and issues with time and timing.

Resistance to Change

In addition to being willing to carry their assigned responsibilities, all three participants need to be open to change and willing to take risks involved with professional growth. Going into the process with a resistance to change by any of the three will greatly lessen the chances of arriving at the insights that could stimulate growth and development. A visiting evaluator will find it difficult to have a fruitful conversation with a teacher who is defensive and not able to be open about struggles, or with a teacher who is comfortably complacent in their work and not interested in trying new things. On the other hand, it will be difficult for the teacher if the evaluator makes a suggestion to change something without first asking the teacher why it was being done in another way. It is possible for the most experienced teacher to learn something from a first-year teacher.

Resistance on the part of the institution can manifest in an evaluation process as a hidden agenda, which may be in the form of a prejudice or an unspoken decision. For example, certain colleagues may have already lost confidence in a teacher's work, but have avoided or been unsuccessful in communicating their concerns. The only purpose of bringing in an evaluator in such a case may be to justify what has already been decided prior to the evaluation visit. If this becomes apparent during the process, it will be difficult for both the evaluator and the educator being observed to feel that they have any real influence on the final outcome of the situation.

Disparity of Expectations

Another set of problems will be encountered when there is a disparity of expectations among the different participants. Does the educator have realistic expectations of themselves in relation to the years of experience and availability of mentoring and support? Are the evaluator's expectations of the same teacher realistic? Are the expectations of the responsible group for the evaluator in line with the evaluator's experience? Does the evaluator have enough experience with children of the age group in the class being observed to offer valid suggestions and recommendations?

If the responsible group has not clearly communicated its expectations to the visiting evaluator, the evaluator's observations will not have the benefit of a full or proper context for the evaluation. From the evaluator's point of view, sometimes an institution's expectations may not be reasonable. For example, an evaluator should not be expected to stay in the home of the teacher being observed or in the home of a teacher who is a member of the group overseeing the evaluation, as this could make it more difficult for the evaluator to maintain the necessary level of objectivity. Problems can also arise when parents who are asked to participate in the evaluation process are not given clear information about what will be done with the feedback about their child's teacher.

Communication Difficulties

The area of communication often presents the greatest challenges. Many evaluators have found that having conversations with the teacher being evaluated before and after the classroom observations was crucial to their ability to make useful recommendations. Educators undergoing evaluation have agreed that these conversations were equally valuable for them. Without these conversations, misunderstandings are much more likely to occur. It can be disheartening for a teacher to read a significant comment in an evaluator's written report that was not spoken about in person, or to hear it from the responsible group without being given an opportunity to respond or give a context to the comment.

In the pre-visit conversation, trust is created when both the evaluator and the teacher being evaluated have the opportunity to speak and to ask questions. Questions might be focused on biographical information or the educator's responses to the Self-Evaluation Questionnaire. Starting the post-visit conversation with a non-judgmental sharing of impressions and observations creates a common ground on which further discussion can be built. Sometimes an evaluator can give a teacher so much feedback that the teacher feels overwhelmed. It is usually much more helpful for the teacher to be given a few specific and concrete recommendations.

Communication around evaluations can be of an extremely delicate nature and it is the responsibility of the group that oversees the professional review in the institution to make sure that unfounded comments, hearsay, and innuendo do not destroy the integrity of the process. If the group meets with the evaluator either before or after the classroom visit, it is preferable that the teacher being evaluated be present. If the teacher is not in attendance, it is important that what is said in those meetings has been already or will be communicated to the teacher. Taking notes at meetings, checking them for accuracy, and distributing them to the attendees helps maintain transparency in the process. When there are legal or other issues, a process separate from the regular evaluation should be used, and in that case, other guidelines around communication may be more appropriate.

Issues of Time and Timing

Time and timing can also be critical in an evaluation process. Whenever the process is rushed there is an increased danger of missed steps, missed communication, and misunderstandings. If an evaluation comes too late in the school year, there may not be enough time for the recommended changes to be made or for a teacher who is leaving to find another job. If a teacher is in a personal crisis, the timely scheduling of a visit by an outside evaluator may allow the teacher to receive enough support to keep the personal situation from adversely affecting the work with the children.

Following up on the recommendations contained in an evaluation report is also a matter of time and timing. In some ways, the real work begins once the evaluation process is completed. Too often, follow-up is the most neglected aspect of the professional review. Follow-up can take many forms, but it must be included. When it is not built into the process, any progress that has been won through everyone's hard work can slip away, and the underlying issues will re-emerge with even greater complexity.

The obstacles and hindrances mentioned above are examples drawn from actual experiences. Even though this list of challenges is far from exhaustive, it may still have the effect of dampening our spirits for review and evaluation. However, the purpose in sharing these examples is not to discourage anyone, but to emphasize how much care and attention is needed to make these processes fruitful. We can all take heart from remembering that we learn more from our mistakes than from what we do well! It can also be heartening to know that in working with review and evaluation processes we are helping to create social forces that are needed for our own development and for the future development of humanity.

Conclusion

Lifelong development is an essential aspect in our journey as Waldorf early childhood educators. Self-reflection is the first step on that path. Through our gifts, whether they are natural or hard-won, we are brought to a place where we can learn and grow.

It is our hope that these thoughts and guidelines on mentoring, professional review, and evaluation will help all educators in becoming more inspired in their work, more worthy of imitation by the children in their care, and more enthusiastic about collaborating with colleagues, especially in finding ways to support one another's continued professional growth.

Appendix:
Forms for Professional Review and Evaluation

The sample questions and checklists included in chapters 15, 16, and 17 are reproduced here as forms that may be scanned, photocopied, and used in a school's evaluation process. They may also be adapted according to a school's individual needs or policies. For example, in the Record of Observations by Evaluator form the term "early childhood educator" or "educator" is used throughout, but a school may prefer to use the term "teacher."

Early Childhood Educator Self-Evaluation, Long Form

Early Childhood Educator Self-Evaluation , Short

Checklist for the Evaluator

Record of Observations by the Evaluator

Evaluation Report

Parent-Child Facilitator Review: Sample Questions for a Record of Observations by Evaluator

Checklist for the Institution

Questions for Colleagues

Questions for Parents

EARLY CHILDHOOD EDUCATOR SELF-EVALUATION QUESTIONNAIRE, LONG FORM

Name of early childhood educator _____

Date _____

Ongoing Self-Development

- Describe your present areas of study and your inner work in relation to your task as an educator. Include a description of how you prepare for your class.

- What questions are you carrying?

- List your professional goals for the year.

- What professional development activities (workshops, conferences, mentoring, visits to other educators) have you undertaken during the last three years?

Cultivating a Mood for the Young Child

- What aspects of your work give you the greatest joy?

- Of what are you most appreciative?

- How is joy manifested in the children and in your day with the children?

- In what ways do gratitude, reverence, and wonder live in the physical and social environment?

Being Worthy of Imitation

- In what ways do you see yourself reflected positively in the mirror of the children's behavior?

- In what area do you have to work consciously every day to be a worthy model for the children?

- In what ways are meaningful adult activities practiced in your classroom?

- In what ways are healthy social relations modeled?

Life-Filled Activity as the Heart of Early Childhood Education

- What is the most creative aspect of the work for you? How do you find renewal for your own creative forces?

- How do you balance practical work, artistic, and play activities for the children? How do you try to balance the needs of the group and the needs of the individuals in your class?

- How can you tell from the children themselves that there is a healthy flow and balance in the structure and rhythms of the day and week?

- Give an example of how the children demonstrate that they are secure enough in their surroundings to bring forth individual creative impulses, especially in play.

Nourishing Growth and Development

- If you are working with a mixed-age group, how do you adjust what you bring and your expectations to the different ages of the children?

- How are you working consciously to support the children's development of the senses of touch, life, movement, and balance?

- In what ways do you experience that the children in your class are thriving?

- Are there individual children about whom you have concerns or questions? How are you addressing these concerns or questions? Do you have the support and/or resources that you need to address them?

Creating a Circle of Warmth and Love

- In what ways are you consciously trying to create warmth, love, and inclusion in the physical environment, in the children's daily activities, in social relations, and in the handling of disruptive or challenging behavior?

- How does this circle include the parents of the children in your care?

- How would you characterize your relations with your colleagues?

- What contribution do you make to the school community as a whole?

The Art of Listening and the Practice of Collaboration

- Describe how you and your colleagues work with child study. How are you honing your skills in child observation?

- How do you deal with conflict in collegial relations or in situations where you disagree with existing decisions or policies?

- What is most rewarding in your work with parents? What is most challenging?

- How are you cultivating a spiritual connection to the children in your care?

Final Questions

- Is there a picture or an image that captures your year, your class, or this process for you?

- What do you hope to gain from this review process?

- Is there anything else that you want to share with others who will be receiving this information?

EARLY CHILDHOOD EDUCATOR SELF-EVALUATION QUESTIONNAIRE, SHORT FORM

Name of early childhood educator _____

Date _____

Ongoing Professional Development

- Describe your present areas of study and your inner work in relation to your task as an educator. Include a description of how you prepare for your class.

- What questions are you carrying?

- List your professional goals for the year.

- What professional development activities have you undertaken in the last three years?

Cultivating a Mood for the Young Child

- In what ways do joy, gratitude, reverence, and wonder live in you and in the environment you have created for the children?

Being Worthy of Imitation

- In what area do you have to work most consciously to be a worthy model for the children?

Life-Filled Activity as the Heart of Early Childhood Education

- How do you balance practical work, artistic, and creative play activities for the children?

Nourishing Growth and Development

- How are you working consciously to support the children's developing senses of touch, life, movement, and balance?

Creating a Circle of Warmth and Love

- In what ways are you trying to create warmth, love, and inclusion in the physical environment, in the daily activities of the children, and for your colleagues and the parents?

The Art of Listening and the Practice of Collaboration

- How do you deal with disagreement or conflict (1) in the classroom with the children, (2) with colleagues, and (3) with parents?

Final Questions

- Is there a picture or an image that captures your year, your class, or this process for you?

- What do you hope to gain from this review process?

- Is there anything else that you want to share with others who will be receiving this information?

CHECKLIST FOR THE EVALUATOR

Preparation for the Visit

- Am I inwardly and outwardly prepared for the evaluation visit?

- Do I have copies of all the relevant material?

- Do I know what the school expects of me?

- Do I know to what group or committee I am responsible?

- Do I know how to reach my contact person (phone and email) at the school?

- Have I read the teacher's self-evaluation?

- Have I set up a phone or email conversation or a meeting with the teacher prior to my visit?

- Do I have a schedule for my visit?

- Am I conscious of the teacher's questions as well as the questions of the school?

Initial Meeting with the Teacher

- How did I help us form a positive working relationship prior to the observation?

- Did we review the teacher's self-evaluation together?

- Did I ask the teacher about additional questions?

- Did I ask the teacher if there was anything that they would like me to observe?

- Was I able to listen without jumping to conclusions?

- Is my interest in this person genuine?

The Classroom Observation

- As I begin my observation, have I made myself inwardly available?

- Did I arrange with the teacher where I should sit and what I should do to be less obtrusive?

- Did I take in impressions without falling into sympathy or antipathy?

- Did I make observations objectively?

- Was I able to be inwardly calm?

- Was I able to bring myself into the right mood for the children?

- Was I a supportive presence for the teacher?

The Post-Observation Conversation

- Were there sufficient time and a private space for an in-depth conversation?

- Did I ask the teacher if the day was typical or not?

- Did I allow the teacher to speak first?

- Did I offer my observations before offering any interpretations?

- Did I ask the teacher to explain why certain things were done as they were?

- Did I share out of my own experiences?

- Did I refrain from overwhelming the teacher with multiple suggestions?

- Was I honest in sharing my concerns?

- Did we agree on concrete objectives?

- Were we able to find, together, a key to the teacher's future development?

The Written Report

- Were my communications clear, professional, and addressed to the appropriate people?

- Did I ask the teacher to review the report for inaccuracies?

- Was there a fair balance of commendations and recommendations in the report?

- Were specific goals, timelines, and support suggested in the report?

- Were options for professional development opportunities noted when appropriate?

- Did I respect agreements for confidentiality?

RECORD OF OBSERVATIONS BY THE EVALUATOR

Name of early childhood educator _____

School or Program _____

Date(s) of visit(s) _____

Name of Evaluator _____

The areas below correlate to the questions in the Self-Evaluation Questionnaire that was completed by the teacher being observed prior to the visit by the outside evaluator. A copy of the completed Self-Evaluation Questionnaire should be attached to the Record of Observations and to the Evaluation Report. Please comment on your observations in the following areas:

Mood for the Young Child

- How is the early childhood educator cultivating a mood of joy, gratitude, wonder, and reverence for the young child? How do these qualities manifest in the educator, in the environment, and in the social life in the class?

Being Worthy of Imitation

- How is the early childhood educator working at being worthy of imitation, both in the areas of natural strengths and gifts and in areas that are more challenging?

Life-Filled Activity

- How does the rhythm of the day provide for a balance of practical work, artistic activity, and creative play? How does the early childhood educator balance the needs of the class and those of individual children?

Nourishing Growth and Development

- How do the children demonstrate that they are thriving? How is the early childhood educator working to help the children develop their senses of touch, life, movement, and balance? Is the diversity that lives among the children acknowledged and worked with in the environment and in everyday activities? Are there developmental needs of individual children or a group of children that appear to need attention?

Creating a Circle of Warmth and Love

- How does the early childhood educator handle social difficulties among the children, or challenging behaviors of individual children? Is there a mood of warmth, inclusivity, and belonging that acknowledges and nourishes the classroom environment, the children, parents, and colleagues? What did you observe about the quality of the relations of the educator with their colleagues and with the parents of the children in the class?

The Art of Listening and the Practice of Collaboration

- How does the early childhood educator demonstrate openness to feedback and advice from colleagues or mentors? Is there a specific area of the work that appears to need further development and support?

Additional Comments by the Evaluator

Signature of Evaluator _____ Date _____

Signature of Early Childhood Educator _____ Date _____

EVALUATION REPORT

Name of early childhood educator _____

School or Program _____

Commendations

Recommendations

Additional Comments

Signature of Evaluator _____ Date _____

Signature of Early Childhood Educator _____ Date _____

PARENT-CHILD FACILITATOR REVIEW: SAMPLE QUESTIONS FOR A RECORD OF OBSERVATIONS BY EVALUATOR

Mood for the Families

How is the early childhood educator cultivating a mood of joy, gratitude, wonder, and reverence for the families in their care? How do these qualities manifest in the educator, in the environment, and in the social health of the group?

Being Worthy of Imitation

How is the early childhood educator working at being worthy of imitation, both in the areas of natural strengths and gifts, and in areas that are more challenging? How are they finding a balance between the roles of model and companion for the parents/caregivers in the class?

Life-Filled Activity

How does the form of the class provide a balanced experience for the children and adults? How does the early childhood educator balance the needs of the individual child and the whole group?

Nourishing Growth and Development

How do the children and families demonstrate that they are thriving? How does the early childhood educator adjust their approach based on the needs of the group or groups that they are carrying?

Creating a Circle of Warmth and Love

How does the early childhood educator handle social difficulties among the children, or challenging behaviors of individual children? What do you observe about the quality of the relations between the educator and the parents/caregivers in the class, and between the educator and their colleagues? How does the early childhood educator provide a mood of warmth, belonging, and inclusivity?

The Art of Listening and the Practice of Collaboration

How does the early childhood educator demonstrate openness to feedback and advice from colleagues or mentors? How does the educator create a listening space for the adults in the class? Is there a specific area of the work that appears to need further development and support?

CHECKLIST FOR THE INSTITUTION

As an institution, we are cultivating a positive climate of review and evaluation and fostering the capacities and skills needed by participating colleagues.

- The faculty and staff are aware of the importance of review and evaluation as a valuable component of teacher development and as a way of being accountable to one another, to the parents and to their community.

- As a group, we practice setting goals and reviewing results when appropriate.

- Our faculty agreements encourage direct communication.

- We practice listening to one another in our meetings.

- We are interested in what is going on in our colleagues' classrooms.

We have established regular rhythms of review and evaluation that assure adequate support for ongoing teacher development.

- Teachers expect to participate in regular cycles of self-evaluation, peer visits, and professional review by an outside evaluator.

- Cycles are accommodated in our meeting schedules and other organizational rhythms.

- Parents and board members are aware of the evaluation timelines and procedures.

- Someone is responsible for scheduling and communication concerning evaluations.

- Consideration is given as to whether it would be beneficial to have the outside evaluator visit for more than one day. Time for conversation with the educator being evaluated is built into the schedule of the outside evaluator's visit.

There is a separate, special policy and procedure for cases of serious concern.

Expectations, timelines, and protocol have been articulated in writing and systems are in place to make sure that the processes are upheld.

- Written policies and procedures for professional review have been distributed to all the early childhood educators and have been discussed in the appropriate collegial groups.

- There is a group who has been mandated to oversee the professional review process.

- Colleagues know where to address questions and concerns about the process.

- There is an established protocol for communication concerning evaluation that has been published and that everyone is expected to follow.

- If parents are asked to participate, they receive clear, written communication about the process and their role. Parents know where to address questions about the process.

- Every outside evaluator has a contact person who makes sure that the evaluator receives all of the relevant materials in a timely way, schedules spaces for meetings, and arranges for the meals and accommodations of the evaluator.

- If there are standard forms for self-evaluations, peer visits, and evaluator reports, these are distributed to those who are expected to complete them by the contact person. Report forms should include space for commendations as well as recommendations.

- There are a process and resources in place for the evaluator to be adequately compensated.

The institution provides support for individual professional development recommended in the written report, including funds for courses, if required.

- The educator being evaluated meets with the responsible group to look over the materials that have been collected. Together, they create a professional development plan for the educator that has specific goals and a timeline.

- Support from the institution may include additional mentoring in a specific area, providing an opportunity to visit another teacher's classroom, or offering funds for a summer course or additional training.

- Professional development funds are available for teachers who need additional training.

- Arrangements for additional follow-up meetings are made if needed.

The institution has adequate mentoring and in-service training opportunities that complement the review and evaluation processes.

- If the teacher being evaluated has a mentor, the mentor should be invited by the responsible group to attend the post-observation conversation or be given a copy of the written report by the teacher.

- Mentors support the teachers they are mentoring by integrating into their mentoring sessions work on the goals articulated in the individual professional development plans.

QUESTIONS FOR COLLEAGUES

Appreciations

- In what ways do you value this colleague?

- What gifts does this colleague bring to the school?

Professionalism

- Give examples of this colleague's professionalism or lack of professionalism, e.g., punctuality, reliability, discretion, and respect for confidentiality.

- How well and in what ways does this colleague represent the school to the parents and in the larger community?

Colleagueship

- Has this colleague demonstrated a willingness to work collaboratively? Give examples.

- Does this colleague support other teachers by sharing resources, experience, and skills? Give examples.

Involvement

- How would you describe this colleague's contributions to meetings?

- To what extent does this colleague take on responsibilities in the school beyond caring for their class? In what ways?

Development

- Is this colleague open to feedback or advice? Give examples.

- How does this colleague deal with conflict?

- Have you experienced this colleague's willingness to work on areas that are challenging?

- How?

Signature of Colleague _____ Date _____

QUESTIONS FOR PARENTS

- Please describe the quality of communication between you and your child's teacher.

- In what ways have you found the class meetings to be valuable?

- In what ways was the parent/teacher conference helpful to you?

- Do you have any other reflections that you would like to share with your child's teacher?

Signature of Parent _____ Date _____

References for Mentoring in Waldorf Early Childhood Education

In addition to the references below, we refer you to further complementary work that has been done by the Association of Waldorf Schools of North America (AWSNA). Register for free and download their "Field Guide for Pedagogical Mentoring in Partnership" on the AWSNA hub at https://community.awsna.org/viewdocument/field-guide-for-pedagogical-mentori-1.

Aasland, Aina, et al. 2020. "Characteristics of Teacher Educators." *Pedagogical Section at the Goetheanum Journal* 69 (Midsummer): 25–28.

Al Huang, Chungliang, and Jerry Lynch. 1995. *Mentoring: The Tao of Giving and Receiving Wisdom*. San Francisco: Harper.

Allen, Paul Marshall and Joan DeRis. 1995. *The Time Is at Hand! The Rosicrucian Nature of Goethe's Fairy Tale of the Green Snake and the Beautiful Lily and the Mystery Dramas of Rudolf Steiner*. Hudson, NY: Anthroposophic Press.

AWSNA, A Colloquium on Developing the Art of Mentoring, 2002, www.awsna.org. (This reference no longer appears online.)

AWSNA Pedagogical Advisors' Colloquium. 2006. *Working Together: An Introduction to Pedagogical Mentoring in Waldorf Schools*. Hudson, NY: AWSNA Publications.

Cunningham, John. *Compassionate Communication and Waldorf Schools*. 2002. N.p.: PuddleDancer Press. Available online as a free PDF.

Fischer, Norman. 2011. *Sailing Home: Using the Wisdom of Homer's Odyssey to Navigate Life's Perils and Pitfalls*. Berkeley, CA: North Atlantic Books.

Goethe, J. W. von. 1979. *The Green Snake and the Beautiful Lily*. No translator listed. New York: SteinerBooks.

Herman, Lee, and Alan Mandell. 2004. *Teaching to Mentoring: Practice, Dialogue and Life in Adult Education*. New York: Routledge/Falmer.

Kühlewind, Georg. 2004. Translated by Pauline Wehrle. *Star Children: Understanding Children Who Set Us Special Tasks and Challenges*. Great Barrington, MA: Temple Lodge.

Mepham, Trevor. 2001. *Teachers Helping Teachers: Mentoring in Steiner Waldorf Schools*. Forest Row, UK: Steiner Waldorf Schools Fellowship.

Pyle, Howard and Katharine. 1965. *The Wonder Clock: Or, Four and Twenty Marvelous Tales, Being One for Each Hour of the Day*. New York: Dover Publications.

Rosenberg, Marshall. 2003. *Nonviolent Communication: A Language of Life—Create Your Life, Your Relationships, and Your World in Harmony with Your Values*. N.p.: PuddleDancer Press.

Smit, Jørgen. 1992. Edited by Natalie Adams, James Pewtherer, and Douglas Gerwin. No translator listed. *The Child, the Teachers, and the Community*. N.p.: Pedagogical Section Council of North America.

Steiner, Rudolf. 1990. *The Riddle of Humanity: The Spiritual Background of Human History*. No translator listed. London: Rudolf Steiner Press.

_____. 1994. *How to Know Higher Worlds*. Translated by Christopher Bamford. Great Barrington, MA: Anthroposophic Press.

_____. 1995a. *The Kingdom of Childhood*. Foundations of Waldorf Education, vol. 21. Original translation by Helen Fox, revised. Great Barrington, MA: Anthroposophic Press.

_____. 1995b. *Self-Education in the Light of Spiritual Science*. Lecture from March 14, 1912, Berlin. No translator listed. Spring Valley, NY: Mercury Press.

_____. 1996a. *The Child's Changing Consciousness as the Basis of Pedagogical Practice*. Foundations of Waldorf Education, vol. 16. Translated by Roland Everett, edited by Rhona Everett. Great Barrington, MA: Anthroposophic Press.

_____. 1996b. *The Education of the Child—and Early Lectures on Education*. Foundations of Waldorf Education, vol. 25. Translated by George and Mary Adams; Robert Lathe and Nancy Whittaker; and Rita Stebbing. Great Barrington, MA: Anthroposophic Press, 1996.

_____. 1997. *An Outline of Esoteric Science*. Translated by Catherine E. Creeger. Great Barrington, MA: Anthroposophic Press.

_____. 2001. *Guidance in Esoteric Training: From the Esoteric School*. No translator listed. Translation revised by C. Davey and O. Barfield, with supplementary material translated by M. Barton, J. Collis, R. Stebbing, and M. Cotterell. London: Rudolf Steiner Press.

_____. 2004a. *A Modern Art of Education*. Foundations of Waldorf Education, vol. 17. Translated by Jesse Darrell, Robert Lathe and Nancy Whittaker, George Adams, and Frederick Amrine. Great Barrington, MA: Anthroposophic Press.

_____. 2004b. *Start Now! A Book of Soul and Spiritual Exercises*. No translator listed. Edited by Christopher Bamford. Great Barrington, MA: SteinerBooks.

_____. 2005. *Verses and Meditations*. Translated by George and Mary Adams. Forest Row, UK: Rudolf Steiner Press.

_____. 2012. *On the Play of the Child: Indications by Rudolf Steiner for Working with Young Children*. Translated by Jan-Kees Saltet. Spring Valley, NY: Waldorf Early Childhood Association of North America.

_____. 2013a. *Spiritual Insights*. Edited by Helmut von Kügelgen. No translator listed. The Little Series. Spring Valley, NY: Waldorf Early Childhood Organization of North America.

_____. 2013b. *The Study of Man*. Translated by Daphne Harwood and Helen Fox, revised and edited by A. C. Harwood. Forest Row, UK: Rudolf Steiner Press.

_____. 2019. *The Essentials of Education*. Translated by Frederick Amrine. Hudson, NY: SteinerBooks/ Anthroposophic Press.

Ueland, Brenda. 1992. "Tell Me More: On the Fine Art of Listening." *Utne Reader* (Nov.–Dec.).

Van Houten, Coenraad. 1999. *Awakening the Will: Principles and Processes in Adult Learning*. Translated by Marianne Krampe. Forest Row, UK: Temple Lodge.

Wheatley, Margaret. 2001. "Listening as Healing." *Shambhala Sun* (Dec.). Available as a free PDF at https://margaretwheatley.com/library/articles/.

Zimmermann, Heinz. 1996. *Speaking, Listening, Understanding: The Art of Creating Conscious Conversation*. Translated by James H. Hindes. Hudson, NY: Lindisfarne Press.

_____. 2003. *Rejuvenating Impulses in Waldorf Education*. Translated by Jo and Christian Reuter. Kelowna, BC, CA: Pegasus Publishing.

About the Authors

Allison Carroll has worked in Waldorf Early Childhood education in San Francisco since 2004 in parent-child, preschool and kindergarten. Before that she worked with international students and families in San Diego, Fort Collins and Boston. Allison was a Rotary Ambassador of Goodwill Scholar to St. Andrews, Scotland, and studied for a year in Galway, Ireland. She has a special interest in DEIJ, outdoor/nature education and fairy/folk tales and has been a member of the Magic Lantern Marionette Troupe since 2007. It has been her great joy to support families as they navigate parenthood and Waldorf education and to continue to learn about human development in the light of Anthroposophy.

Diane David was among the founding parents of the San Francisco Waldorf School, where she worked for twenty-eight years as a kindergarten teacher and was strongly mentored by some amazing teachers. She still teaches parent-child classes at SFWS. She is the Director of Early Childhood at the Bay Area Center for Waldorf Teacher Training and active in WECAN, both as a member of the Teacher Education Committee and as co-representative for Northern California. She is a mentor and evaluator committed to building strong Waldorf schools through foundational work in early childhood.

Louise deForest taught in the Waldorf kindergarten for many years, then spent fifteen years as an international educational consultant, traveling around the world every year offering lectures, workshops, and engaging in teacher training. She served on the WECAN board for twenty years. Now "retired," Louise is one of two North American representatives on the Council of the International Association of Steiner/ Waldorf Early Childhood Education.

Nancy Foster was a Waldorf early childhood teacher for over thirty years at Acorn Hill Waldorf Kindergarten and Nursery in Silver Spring, Maryland, where she taught kindergarten, nursery, and parent-child classes. She also served as a mentor for teachers and as a visiting speaker at Waldorf schools, offered workshops at conferences, and taught in the early childhood teacher education program at Sunbridge Institute in Spring Valley, New York. Nancy has published two collections of seasonal music and verse: *Let Us Form a Ring* and *Dancing as We Sing*. She also edited the WECAN publications *Mentoring in Waldorf Early Childhood Education*, *The Seasonal Festivals in Waldorf Early Childhood Education*, and *The Mood of the Fifth: A Musical Approach to Early Childhood*.

Nancy and her husband, a retired professional musician, live in Washington, DC. They encountered Waldorf education and anthroposophy while seeking a school for their two sons, now grown.

Andrea Gambardella has been serving Waldorf early education since 1975. Andrea directed the Sunbridge College (now Institute) full-time early childhood educators program and has taught mixed-age kindergarten, preschool, and parent-child classes. She served on the WECAN board, on the AWSNA Leadership Council, and in leadership roles for Green Meadow and Baltimore Waldorf schools. Andrea continues to mentor teachers, serve as a site visitor to schools and training centers, and cares deeply for the rights of the young child and the future of Waldorf education. She is the mother of three Waldorf graduates.

Susan Howard has been active in WECAN since its founding 1984, first as a board member, and later as Coordinator and Co-director. She was the Director of the Early Childhood Teacher Education program at Sunbridge College from 1984–2002 and the part-time Early Childhood Teacher Education program at Sunbridge Institute until 2018. Susan also serves as a Co-Coordinator of the International Association for Steiner/Waldorf Early Childhood Education based in Dornach, Switzerland, and is a member of its Council and its Working Group on Teacher Education. She lives in Amherst, Massachusetts, with her husband Michael, an artist, researcher, and author.

Holly Koteen-Soulé worked as a Waldorf Early Childhood Teacher and Parent and Child Leader for twenty-five years. She is a founding member of Sound Circle Center for Arts and Anthroposophy in Seattle, served as its Early Childhood Director for twenty years and is currently the Center's Early Childhood Program Advisor. She is a member of the WECAN Teacher Education committee. She is also a member of the Pedagogical Section Council of North America and the WECAN Early Childhood Research Group. Holly has an MA in Education from Antioch University in Seattle and has written and edited many articles on Waldorf education.

Carol Nasr Griset has taught young children for fifteen years, pioneering the nursery program at the Toronto Waldorf School and working in the parent-tot program. Later she led the Halifax Waldorf Playgroup, a home-based program in Nova Scotia. Also in Halifax, she taught adults in an ECE program at a community college and led parent-child classes at a single-parent center. She currently lives with her husband in Orange County, California, where she teaches parent-child and parent-infant classes. Carol is training with RIE (Resources for Infant Educarers) and has completed RIE II. She mentored for Rudolf Steiner College in the early childhood education programs and for LifeWays. In addition, she works as a pediatric chaplain in a children's hospital and as a mentor to parents of young children. She is the mother of five grown children and has recently become a grandmother.

Anna Rainville has been a Waldorf educator since 1978. She now travels widely to mentor and teach. Her experience as a class teacher, a kindergarten teacher, and with adult learners continues to delight and deepen her interest in Waldorf education. Whether in classrooms, living rooms, zoom rooms, conferences, teacher training centers, universities, or forest schools, Anna enjoys supporting teachers, both new and seasoned. Anna lives in California and works nationally and internationally, in regions including the Philippines, Estonia, the West Bank, Ireland, and India. Special interest in learning through movement and sensory integration led her to complete remedial training. Her book, *Singing Games for Families, Schools and Communities*, is cherished by early childhood teachers.

Kim Raymond has been involved with Waldorf Education for over thirty years and has the distinction of being a graduate of the first teacher training class at Rudolf Steiner College in Fair Oaks, California. After many years of teaching kindergarten at the Sacramento Waldorf School, she moved to Santa Monica during a sabbatical year to help expand the early childhood programs at Westside Waldorf School. During her five years there she served as an officer on the Board of Directors and as Head of Faculty. For the past six years she has been teaching kindergarten on the beautiful island of Maui at the Haleakala Waldorf School. Kim is the WECAN Regional Representative for Hawaii and taught early childhood education in the Summer Teacher Education program at Rudolf Steiner College. She has three grown daughters, all Waldorf graduates, and has recently become a doting grandma.

Celia Riahi has been teaching and caring for young children for most of her life. She began working as a nanny during her teenage years, and opened The Other Mother, a Waldorf-inspired home daycare program, when her only daughter, now grown, was fourteen months old. She ran this program for ten years and then taught kindergarten at the Rudolf Steiner School in New York City for four years. She later taught kindergarten at the Hartsbrook School in Hadley, Massachusetts, for eighteen years. Celia currently lives with her wife in Amherst, Massachusetts; together, they have run the Cottage Garden, a Waldorf home day care for children aged ten months to three years old, for the past seventeen years. Celia has also worked as a jeweler, sculptor, and fiber artist, and studied painting at the Rudolf Steiner Institute, where she was a board member and managed the bookstore.

Patricia Rubano is a mother and grandmother living in San Diego, who became an early childhood educator in 1974 and became involved with Waldorf education in 1977. Patricia has worked with children from infancy through age seven. She was part of the founding group of the Waldorf School of San Diego and has worked in and with both initiative and established schools. She currently offers mentoring and evaluation for early childhood programs and sometimes serves as adjunct faculty in teacher training programs. She has been a faculty member and director for the Biography and Social Arts Certificate Program for many years (visit the Center for Biography and Social Art online for more information), and brings workshops for all members of Waldorf communities on many themes, but always with the goal of "Awakening Connections Within and With Others."

Susan Silverio directed, taught, and mentored the LifeWays East Coast Part-Time Early Childhood Training from 2006–2013. She was the founding teacher of Ashwood Waldorf School in Rockport, Maine, and led a mixed-age kindergarten for twenty-eight years near the architectural studio and homesteads of her husband and stepson. Susan also founded and directed Mid-Coast Hospitality House, a temporary and emergency shelter that now develops affordable housing in the MidCoast area as Homeworthy. Since her retirement, Spindlewood continues as a preschool on the land near her home, in the care of a LifeWays and Waldorf trained teacher. Susan continues to garden.